"*The YES Frequency* is an e[...] formation. Gary educates, [...] derful read for anyone intere[...] the self."
— Don Miguel Ruiz, *New York Times* best-selling author of *The Four Agreements*

"What an important subject, and what an amazing book. Gary Quinn has hit a home run with this ... and the timing is perfect. I can't think of a better way to bring massive attention to the single word that can change the world.
— James F. Twyman, author of *The Moses Code* and *Emissary of Light*

"*The YES Frequency* is a simple 'how to' guide to impact and spiritually transform your life. To be conscious you must be willing to be present each moment of each day. The word 'YES' is energy enlisting that support. This book will help break down positive practices, 'How do you get to Carnegie Hall?'... the processes of manifesting your desires to live in a world of great possibility. This book can help you on that path. Make the commitment to a lasting change! Make everywhere you go better because you were THERE!"
— Greg Louganis, USA Diving Olympic gold medalist, 1984 & 1988, and author of *Breaking the Surface*

"As someone who always believed in the power of positive thinking, despite all evidence to the contrary, I applaud Gary's optimistic and delightfully spiritual approach to saying yes to this magical life of ours. Let Gary show you the power of saying yes!"
— W. Bruce Cameron, author of *A Dog's Purpose*

"Gary Quinn's inspired message of love, continues to illuminate and enhance one's spiritual journey with joy and hope!"
— Dyan Cannon, Academy Award–nominated actress, author of *Dear Cary: My Life with Cary Grant*

"Gary always has the pulse on how you can achieve your best life through being YOU. I am always inspired by his words and his great guidance!"
— Mariel Hemingway, Academy Award–nominated actress, author of *The Willing Way* and *Healthy Living from the Inside Out*

"Yes, what a powerful word. Gary Quinn has done so much with that simple, yet oh so powerful world. "Say YES to life"! Thank you, Gary, for providing us with this perfectly timed book that will enhance the lives of so many.   — Linda Gray, actress, *Dallas* television show

"Gary Quinn is an extraordinary teacher of wisdom, vision, and heart. *The YES Frequency* holds the keys to what you really want. Books like this change lives and the world. Let it bless you!"
      — Alan Cohen, author of *Enough Already: The Power of Radical Contentment*

"*The YES Frequency* is an extraordinary book! Stepping into the vibration of "Yes" can powerfully transform every aspect of your life. In this inspiring and remarkable book, Gary Quinn takes you to the core of how to create an awe-inspired life. It works! I highly recommend this book."
                                    — Denise Linn, best-selling author of *Sacred Space*

"*The YES Frequency* helps readers to uncover their untapped power, synchronicity and intuition. This book will help you understand yourself, define what you want, and give you the tools to create it."
      — John Holland, author of *The Spirit Whisperer: Chronicles of a Medium*

"*The YES Frequency* is a powerfully uplifting guide that will lead you straight into a positive, compassionate, and truly happy state of mind. Gary's simple, direct, and practical wisdom will no doubt affect every reader in a profoundly beneficial way."
                              — Nicolai Bachman, author of *The Path of the Yoga Sutras*

"Stop looking in the wrong places and asking the wrong questions. The *YES Frequency* is the book you were looking for. Uncover your untapped power NOW."
      — Mabel Katz, international speaker and author of *The Easiest Way to Live*

"Let Gary take you on a journey of your life and you just might not want to come back!"
                                              — Eric Pearl, author of *The Reconnection*

"*The YES Frequency* creates a vibration that parts the clouds above allowing the inspiration of the light of the sun to empower and guide us. The teachings in this book help us to ride the wave to the best that life has to offer. Gary Quinn's work is brilliant and inspiring!!"

— Sandra Ingerman, author of *Soul Retrieval* and *Medicine for the Earth*

"If you want to stay young and optimistic, read *The YES Frequency*. The practical tools that Gary Quinn outlines in this book will keep you in the positive zone so that you can manifest creativity and joy for the rest of your life!"

— Caroline Sutherland, author of *The Body Knows ... How to Stay Young*

"*The YES Frequency* is an engaging guide that can dramatically transform, empower and enrich your life forever. Gary Quinn teaches you how to gain clarity, using his simple and essential strategies. This book will help you take control of your life, change your thinking and create the life you really want. A must read!"

— Debbie Meyer, USA Swimming, three-time individual Olympic gold Medalist, 1968

"Gary Quinn has done a remarkable job of distilling ideas that have been around for hundreds of years and making them relevant to today. He has also broken some new ground with some outstanding ideas of his own."

— Charlie Matthau, film director

"Survival behavior is related to one's ability to say no to the world and the things you do not want to do and yes to yourself and the things you want to do. If you say no to yourself your body and life will suffer the consequences. *The YES Frequency* can help you to create your YES life."

— Bernie Siegel, MD, author of *Love, Medicine, and Miracles*, *365 Prescriptions For The Soul*, and *A Book of Miracles*

"*The YES Frequency* offers a complete program for discovering your deepest heartfelt desires and manifesting them."

— Arielle Ford, author of *The Soulmate Secret*

"*The YES Frequency* eloquently defines my favorite word, BELIEF ... its power and contagion essential to navigating, enjoying and succeeding in today's warp-speed world. With repetition, silently and audibly, I encourage all fortunate readers to simply say YES, BELIEVE in the BELIEF of our spiritual universe and the endless messages it provides. Many thanks to Gary for sharing his experiences and wisdom so that others may fully recognize, hear and utilize the many gifts of everyday Divine Enlightenment."

– Jeff Float, USA Swimming gold medalist, 1984

"Stunning! A book of wisdom and power. Say YES to it!"

– Dr. Joe Vitale, author of *Attract Money Now*

"Gary Quinn has given you a step-by-step process to live the empowered and expansive life that is your destiny."

– Cynthia James, author of *What Will Set You Free* and *Revealing Your Extraordinary Essence*

"You may be familiar with the expression 'the universe is whispering to you.' It encourages us to listen to this powerful source in the midst of today's blizzard of technology. Gary Quinn's revolutionary, yet simple technique illustrates how to achieve this, embodied in the simple word YES. On a very deep level, this wonderful book will simply change your life!"

– Glennyce Eckersley, author of *An Angel to Guide Me*

"This book has taught me that YES matters. In a world where it is so easy to be overwhelmed by negativity, concentrating on positive energy and surrounding yourself with love will change the course of your life – and how much you enjoy it."

– Ilyce Glink, author of *Buy, Close, Move In!*, nationally syndicated columnist

"Gary Quinn is a rare teacher with such heart, a voice for our times."

– Maggie Hamilton, author of *Love Your Work: Reclaim Your Life*

"*The YES Frequency* helps you identify and develop a positive belief system that will allow you to step out of "the past, the lack, the limitations," and create a powerful new blueprint using the word 'YES'. This book is a great guide for living, and I would recommend it to anyone who is looking to improve their life!"
   – Robert Kovacik, Emmy Award–winning journalist, co-anchor of NBC News

"In Life it should always be about "Yes, and..." instead of "No Way". *The Yes Frequency* allows you to find your inner channel to truly connect with your deep desire of turning your life into a success and achieve the happy destiny of your dreams. Become Peace in Action and connect yourself to the right frequency, the only one, the Yes Frequency".
   – Emmanuel Itier, film director, *The Invocation*

"*The YES Frequency* is a touchstone of essential information for anyone wanting to achieve great change. Gary gives you the tools to manifest your true desires, access our built-in supply of love, energy and knowledge by using the power of "YES". A very inspirational book, and in tune with our needs today."
   – Richard Ayoub, Emmy Award–winning television producer

"*The YES Frequency* delivers simple steps to feel more connected, spiritually grounded, and bring you closer to who YOU are truly meant to be."
   – Richard Moss, MD, author of *Inside-Out Healing: Transforming Your Life Through the Power of Presence* and *The Mandala of Being*

"*The YES Frequency* gives you the tools to create and heal your own life. Follow these simple steps and let yourself become what you have always imagined!"
   – Richard Cole, author of *Stairway to Heaven: Led Zeppelin Uncensored*

"There is but one word that brings joy to everyone's ears, YES! Gary Quinn has channeled that word beautifully in *The YES Frequency*. This remarkable book takes you out of the negativity of your NO life, and shows you quite clearly what is possible in your new, YES life! A wonderful journey is guaranteed by all."
   – Judson Rothschild, author of *Snap Out of It! A Quick Guide To Overcoming Panic and Anxiety*

"Say YES to life and life says YES to you! In his inspiring book Gary teaches you important codes to leave blocks and self-sabotaging mechanisms behind you and to learn to live in *The YES Frequency* to manifest the dreams of your life! You have the choice — so say YES to your life!"

— Isabelle von Fallois, author of *The Power of Your Angels*

"With The YES Frequency, Gary Quinn gives us an intriguing method that shows how to connect with the invisible force that surrounds us and, once joined with, can lead one to the optimal expression of love, happiness, and abundance. I highly recommend this book to all who seek a better understanding of how the universe we appear to live in operates."

— Gary Renard, author of *The Disappearance of the Universe and Your Immortal Reality*

"A fundamental spiritual truth is that we are the powerful creators of all we experience. And we create through vibration — including the vibrations of what we say and think. Before we are born, each of us is well aware of this truth, but we forget it upon coming into body. Gary Quinn is here to remind us. Truly, positive speech and thought can have a seemingly magical effect on your life, and *The YES Frequency* can help you tap into that magic."

— Robert Schwartz, author of *Your Soul's Gift: The Healing Power of the Life You Planned Before You Were Born*

"*The YES Frequency* is filled with inspiring simple strategies that make change possible. Gary Quinn offers a step-by-step, no nonsense program for discovering and implementing practical solutions to break old ideas all about changing others, it's about changing you too and restructuring your belief system. A very effective book to help you develop your own inner power!"

— Lee Holden, DOM, author *of 7 Minutes of Magic*, and Qi Gong expert.

The Yes Frequency

The Yes Frequency

Master a Positive Belief System
and Achieve Mindfulness

GARY QUINN

FINDHORN PRESS

First published by Findhorn Press 2013

ISBN 978-1-84409-635-0

British Library Cataloguing-in-Publication Data:
A catalogue record for this book is available from the British Library.

Edited by Nicky Leach
Cover design by Deanna Estes and Thierry Bogliolo
Interior design by Geoff Green Book Design, Cambridge
Printed and bound in the USA

Published by
Findhorn Press
117-121 High Street
Forres IV36 1AB
Scotland, UK

t +44(0)1309 690582
f +44(0)131 777 2711
e info@findhornpress.com
www.findhornpress.com

There is a frequency that surrounds us. It vibrates life into all aspects of the universe. When you understand how to engage your frequency, your life will plug into abundance, success, and contentment. —Gary Quinn

Contents

Part Two: Reconfigure Your Behavior

Part Three: Living Your Vision

Introduction

Welcome to The YES Frequency! When you step into this holistic "frequency," your life will transform to such a radiant degree that the changes will feel like a form of rebirth, uplifting your life. This is a complete guide to how to get your mind to join the party of successful living. Think of it as a kind of hybrid education that will motivate you to move forward in your life. The YES Frequency will allow you to achieve new levels of contentment, using positive reinforcement to create your dreams and goals.

This is no secret. Many people have written about the subject of consciousness over the centuries. My unique talents lie in how I communicate what I call The YES Frequency.

In this book, I will share my translation of The YES Frequency, using some of the techniques I've acquired over years of study. Some of you may recognize parts of my life from prior books, but through The YES Frequency I will uncover some deeper meanings and share them with you. Many pupils and spiritual teachers have encouraged me to share these teachings. The principles are simple, straightforward, and understandable.

My gifts are intuitive. I tap into energy vibrations emanating from individuals, as well as the combined vibrations of a roomful of people, which can be either positive or negative, thereby affecting the experience. After many hours of training in these skills, I have been able to tap into a frequency that has the power to change the ordinary into the extraordinary.

Let me share with you one of my first revelations of this kind, and how it unfolded.

During a trip to Germany, I was scheduled to lecture to a group of people. Normally, when I come onstage to speak, I'm received with the feeling of "open arms." When I took center stage at this particular venue, however, the room radiated such a powerful vibration of "weighted negativity" that I was nearly unable to communicate. Understand: when I lecture I allow a kind of natural osmosis to prevail. I don't come with planned or rehearsed speeches; none of my lectures is the same. Instead, there is a divine intervening communication that I allow to come through me.

This particular day, that divine communication was being hampered. I felt blocked from the natural flow that is usually readily available to me, so I stood in silence for an unnatural beat. The energy of the room was such a low-energy frequency that for a moment I felt stunned.

I took a deep breath and requested assistance from the universe. As I exhaled slowly, I heard my intuitive voice instruct me to allow my positive powers to wash over me and spill into the room. The intuitive voice bade me ask the entire room to take a deep breath and to simply repeat after me: "Yes," and again "Yes," and again "YES."

After each and every "yes," the weight of the room's vibration lifted to a higher frequency, radiating energy of positivity. Like a game of ping-pong, "yes" bounced from me to the people in the room. This "yes" frequency uplifted and lightened the room to such a degree that everyone was in a beautiful choir of "YES."

I share this true story in the hope that it will help guide you in raising your own inner frequency of "Yes." Once you feel The YES Frequency, you will never return to the mundane. The gifts and miracles are everlasting.

Nothing I'm saying is new in the universe, but how I gather and translate this information and share it with you is. I use my gifts to convey to you the touchstones of The YES Frequency by sharing my personal experiences. Please receive this with an open heart. I ask that you listen as a great actor does, then take from this what you will and make it your own.

My words have many layers. They merely come through me. The moment I step onstage my mind is clear. In a manner of speaking, I am just a catalyst for expression. Should we have the opportunity to be in the same room, the energy of the room dictates the exchange. I'm more of a conduit than anything – I allow the energy to come through me and suggest the subject of conversation, trusting the positive inner voice.

I believe that lessons come in various guises. Every one of us has an individual fingerprint, and it is my intention to reach everyone on an individual basis. In order to do this, I must strive to be a kind of nonpartisan speaker and embrace all. My gifts are best received in person, but it is my hope that by consolidating the information they convey in one place, this guide will uplift your life.

At the core of The YES Frequency is my Touchstone for Life™ coaching program. This systematic process facilitates emotional healing while removing the limits and obstacles standing in the way of your dreams. Through using the word "yes," exercises, questions, self-examination, and affirmations, you will learn to free yourself from old negative thoughts and emotions. Using these tools, you will learn to heal your life, rebuild your confidence, and restore your inner strength. Imagine the possibilities when you reach your highest potential and experience this healing frequency.

If we pay attention to the amount of negative chatter that runs through our minds on a daily basis, is it any wonder most of us do not have this spiritual well-being? So much of the time, we are using "limiting" words that connect us to old behavior. My goal is to show you how to change this destructive behavior by simply connecting the dots.

At our core, we have Values and Beliefs. Our lives consist of Goals, Behavior, Emotions, Situations, and Thoughts. If our Values and Beliefs do not align with our Goals, Behaviors, Emotions, Situations, and Thoughts, what happens? Anarchy. If we change our Behavior but continue to feed off our past Emotions and Thoughts, we create the same patterns and situations. If we only alter our Thoughts and Emotions, but our Behavior remains the same, there will be no transformation. In order to effect change we need to make sure that our entire value system is in alignment.

In order to ignite The YES Frequency, you will need to make sure that you are not defeating your core Values and Beliefs. This book will help identify where the breakdown in the alignment is happening, and help you to discover the best of you.

So how do we go about getting in synch with this "frequency" and experiencing all the wonderful blessings that come with it, while rebuilding the best of you? The answer to this question is more meaningful than ever, because we are in an age of technological advancement, multitasking, fifty-two-hour work weeks, and text-a-holics.

This book is about helping you create an amazing life, one in which you feel truly inspired and excited about living. Does this seem like something impossible for you to achieve? By introducing you to The YES Frequency technique, I am going to help you develop a positive belief system that will allow you to step out of the past, the future, the lack, and the limitations, and in doing so create a powerful mission statement for your life. Think of it as a "fast pass" to the frequency of things moving into place. I'll also help you understand how powerful a tool this is in helping to restore your true self by achieving mindfulness. I will help you reconnect the power of self and your true identity.

It all starts with you. As you begin to modify your thoughts, words, and actions, you will begin to change the way you feel about yourself. I will show you how you have created the person you are, and how to create the very best of you.

Whether you realize it or not, your life is directed by the choices you make. This book is designed to teach you how to become more conscious of creating these choices, leading you out of the fear and the illusion in which most people live. You will learn how to break through barriers, forgive, let go, and heal the past. You will become focused and peaceful. Clarity will replace confusion. This will allow you to regain your personal power and allow your frequency to lead you to success.

In my first book, *May the Angels Be With You*, I referred to the story of the Wizard of Oz. You have always had the ability (or the magical shoes, in Dorothy's case) to find your way home. Just like the wizard, I will show you that you have had the power all along. I'm just showing you the steps—*you* will walk the walk. The choice is yours. Stepping into this Frequency of YES is a shortcut to understanding how the universe operates.

As you come to understand the power of choice, you will discover that you will be more open to welcoming good things, people, and opportunities into your life. In my second book, *Living in the Spiritual Zone*, I wrote about the flow of unlimited energy, ideas, love, trust, and the power that exists in the universe. This can only be achieved when we are living consciously and working with these principles.

Stepping inside the Frequency of YES is a " vibrational " strategy that will create the "new you" that you have been looking for. These tools will help you align your subconscious and your conscious mind, which will nourish your spirit and soul.

Every day, we have the opportunity to think, speak, and live consciously. When negative thoughts float into our consciousness we can replace them with positive thoughts. We can also catch ourselves using old, habitual patterns of speaking that might produce lack and limitation, and rephrase our speech to produce abundance and unlimited potential for our lives. Living consciously in this way continually fills our experiences.

The practical information in each chapter is designed to encourage you to engage creatively with your situation, to give you more insight, courage, and harmony in your life, including the freedom to let go of things that aren't working for you; to ask for what you deserve to experience; and to be the kind of person you know you should be. (Please don't be afraid of failing, or of doing any of the exercises wrong—that's impossible!) I would like to add that—as the title suggests—the whole concept of this book is based on the principle of believe and receive. Join the journey of amazing results using the word YES.

When I was working on this book, it seemed like a logical step to combine special affirmations to add to the word YES. As you will see, these words and their properties are connected to demanding areas of modern life that sometimes require a touch of extra inspiration. So many people are looking for a little guidance and support, and I fervently hope it will be found within these pages.

The YES Frequency is within you. Allow me to escort you to tap into it. Let's begin!

Part One
Taking Control Of Your Life

1

The Yes Frequency

There is not a vibrational frequency inside your words, similar to the way your voice has a particular tone and the music of your tone influences how people react to you. The vibration and a frequency inside your words dictates how the universe perceives your intentions.

In teaching The YES Frequency, and searching for how best to formulate and share this technique, I first thought it pertinent to consider the word YES itself . So I pulled out a dictionary, and here is the definition of the word:

Yes (ys) *adv.*

It is so; as you say or ask. Used to express affirmation, agreement, positive confirmation, or consent. *n. pl.* yes·es

1. An affirmative or consenting reply.

2. An affirmative vote or voter.

tr.v. yessed, yes·sing, yes·es

To give an affirmative reply to.

interj.

Used to express great satisfaction, approval, or happiness.

It is interesting to read the actual definitions of the words we use every day. The techniques I use in this book will unravel the patterns of your vocabulary and show you how every single word you choose now forecasts your future. What awaits you if you are willing to trust the unlimited frequency of YES will be an extraordinarily rewarding life, one that has unlimited possibilities. The YES Frequency embodies all the "hopes and dreams" of your life.

We are not talking about saying yes to any negative issues, situations, or happenings—obviously, that would be counter-productive. The mind is a complicated animal; it is always try-ing to make a judgment or attachment to each thought and experience, cataloguing it as a good or bad one. We need to move beyond this instinct.

Trusting the frequency experience of YES creates a powerful force inside you. The oneness we all long for is in this experi-ence. It is not based on who we are, what we have, or where we think we are going in the future; it is based on the truth that we are divine beings, part of the powerful force that lies within us, the same force that creates the beauty of our earth and the infinite universe in which we reside.

Consciously or unconsciously, we are all in alignment with this loving force. The YES Frequency is in this moment—not yesterday's moment and not tomorrow's, but within this very moment. We develop habits and levels of trust based on the conditions of our past, but embracing the moment we find our-selves in takes more than this. We must be willing to transform and heal the past, so that we can truly live in the present.

You need to be aligned emotionally to be connected to The YES Frequency. This isn't as hard as it sounds. You already have the ability to be aligned this way and to tap into The YES Frequency; you just do not know how to unlock it yet.

Let me introduce you to the word YES. YES gives off a great vibration. YES gives off an energy that lights up your being from the inside out. Imagine what your current life would be if you allowed YES to rule not only this moment but the day and the week. I know you will be quite surprised by the results.

Take a moment and think how you feel when you hear the word YES. For most of us, it is uplifting for all the obvious reasons. Doesn't it seem, though, as if we live more often in a world of NO? In this book, we will explore the difference between these two seemingly simple words, and examine why they have such a profound and powerful effect on our emotions, our bodies, our beliefs, and our spirit throughout our entire lives.

Learning to live in The YES Frequency may seem like a Utopian dream. Most of us can think of everyday situations and needs in our daily lives that do not lend themselves to an unqualified YES in any way. We want more of something, or less of something, or maybe just something different, and we do not get that YES feeling about any of it. In many aspects of our lives, NO seems to be the largest feeling.

As our personal wish lists emerge in our minds, our desires become clearer and we review our innermost dreams. Often we hear NO even from our own quiet, internal response. We live from the inside out. What we think and feel internally colors our perspective, our experience, and our belief systems in the outer world.

NO has become synonymous with what we call "reality." We can justify NO with pragmatism. Be "real": you know we cannot have, do, and be that—whatever that is that we wish to be when we listen to the dreams inside ourselves. In this "realistic" space, we incorporate NO into our internal vocabulary almost from birth.

Some of these NO responses come from well-meaning people who care deeply about us, from our social groups and cultures, which define the rules and regulations of expected behavior. After many years of well-practiced repetition, we eventually internalize the NO, which in most cases profoundly affects our subconscious in a negative way. At some point, this answer becomes spontaneous—an unconscious instant response.

NO signifies an absolute sense of limitation, but YES represents an open field of possibilities. YES resonates within and places you in tune with The YES Frequency. It creates endless possibilities, offering a lifeline to a more expansive, unlimited, and fulfilling world. In the chapters ahead, I will teach you how to incorporate a new attitude of YES into your daily life.

YES is a magic word—especially in English. I haven't found any foreign language equivalents that have the same uplifting energy change that the English word YES gives. Repeat YES! Get yourself in a comfortable, uncluttered, quiet place, and for three minutes, just say YES, over and over: YES, YES, YES... Just by repeating this word, you will feel a gentle uplifting of your spirit.

I have seen it work over and over again. For example, I had a client who was in a bad situation. I told her to repeat YES a thousand times every day for seven days. Guess what happened on the seventh day? Miracles started happening—energy shifted, everything changed, because she altered her subconscious mind. She shifted her frequency, and by doing so was able to receive positive changes. After those seven days, she said to me, "If I can do this, anyone can."

People all over the world have changed their lives, just by repeating the word YES. I have no idea why it works—I don't ask, I just trust, because I have seen it work wondrous transformations. It has taken me five years of extensive reading and face-to-face experience, and the results are exhilarating to witness. And not just on a personal level—you will see how The YES Frequency affects those around you as well.

First, monitor your own responses to everything. Observe both your internal dialogue and your verbal statements. Practice thinking and saying YES. Repeat YES, YES, YES! Just feel the energy of the word, and observe how that energy feels within yourself. Where does it register in your body? How does it affect your emotional state, your actions, your energy and vitality? Say it out loud! Repeat it multiple times, and monitor your own reaction; feel it both internally and externally. Notice that you have a YES Frequency vibration and energy that is positive and open when you say YES. Learn to feel the difference, and apply YES as often as you can throughout the day.

Next, take action. This step involves changing some of your old, ingrained habits. Pay special attention to your speech. Hear every word you say, and express a YES moment in as many situations as possible throughout the day. If negative thinking or responses sneak in, replace those thoughts and words with a YES. In this way, we can begin to notice old habitual patterns of speaking, which can produce lack and limitation. Adapt to the YES principle, rephrasing the way you speak to reflect new attitudes of unlimited potential. Instead of NO (I cannot do that, afford that, have that, arrange that, and so on), replace it with a YES, even though the YES may take you into a new and unknown realm. We can all learn new ways of being!

When any of those old words, attitudes, or behaviors arise in you, replace them immediately with new words, thoughts, and actions. This step requires discipline and consciousness; this is where we begin laying the foundation for new learning and introducing the initial process of unraveling the secret to opening your first door to enter The YES Frequency. Enhance your aura and its energetic vibrations, which will enable you to stay present and participate with love.

You are the leader of your life. I will teach you how to write your own life story and be the protagonist.

YES, my positive attitude reigns.

Everything will work out for the highest good. In speaking and relating only to your positive thoughts, please appreciate yourself, your body, and your entire being. You are limitless and infinite. All of life can be seen as love. We are the source and supplier of an abundance of love. Love is the essence of what we are in the world.

Finding My Way

Whether you are attending one of my seminars or are in the midst of reading this book, you are beginning to question the way you are envisioning and living your life. You are analyzing the addition of events that have led you to contemplate today. This is really good! This is a beautiful start to learning this new language of living. I am going to remind you about this over and over. Why? Because it works!

As I share these important tools with you, I will be using the examples and experiences from my own life that served as the catalysts for this technique. As you experience my story, I hope you will reflect on your own life and work to hone your ability.

I first discovered my intuitive gifts as a young boy. When I was about eight years old, I had a strong impression every day, much to my dismay, about a boy I went to school with. We were in the same class, but we did not have much in common, as I was rather introverted as a child and this boy was buoyant and outspoken. He was very nice, though, and I couldn't understand why I was experiencing this undercurrent of knowledge that he was not long for this earth.

It wasn't something I spoke of – it was just that when I saw him every day, as I looked at him, a kind of "flash of time" would jump into my vision and he would vanish from right in front of me. It was an image of dissipation, and each day that I saw him in class that year the dissipation happened faster and faster.

The next year, when I returned to class, I heard from our teacher that he had died over the summer. My feelings were very confusing, and I didn't quite know how to process them. I was in shock and couldn't believe that he had actually died from a car accident, as my visions about him had never depicted the actual accident. Even though everything about this was disconcerting, I did what I could to put it behind me. I took up a new hobby, one of my first loves: swimming.

My family moved many times when I was young, because my stepfather was in the army. At thirteen, I decided to take my swimming seriously and train with the best. My mother was a positive reinforcing support; she sought and found Olympic swim coaches Sherm Chavoor and Mark Schubert, who trained Mark Spitz, Debbie Meyer, Brian Goodell, and Shirley Babashoff – all Olympic gold medal winners.

Without the support of my mother and her belief in me, I'm not so sure I would have pursued my goals at this young age. This was a period of hard work, determination, travel, competing, and gaining confidence in the international sports world. I set many swim records and achieved Junior National status.

In 1976, I graduated high school and journeyed away from Northern California, leaving home and moving to Orange County to train with Mark Shubert's swim club (the Mission Viejo Nadadores). Disappointment came soon after, when, because the United States was boycotting the Russian Olympic games, we were not able to qualify for the USA Olympic team. The boycott of the 1980 Summer Olympic Games in Moscow was part of a package of actions initiated by the United States to protest the Soviet war in Afghanistan. Still, all of us on that swim team felt the weight of that disappointment.

With a heavy heart, I decided instead to take an opportunity to train some actors who needed to work on their swim techniques in order to compete on the television series, *Battle of the Network Stars.* My goals changed as new doors began to open; I moved to Hollywood and became entrenched in the entertainment business. Even as the outside aspects of my life changed, however, I kept my spirituality at the forefront. I was so open and willing to learn that many people gravitated to my pure energy. This was not always well received, although many people appreciated it, and soon I began to find myself serving as a kind of spiritual "guide" for many of my friends.

I remember one day, when I was twenty-five, visiting the Santa Anita Racetrack in Los Angeles with some friends who loved to gamble on the horse races. One friend's stepfather had private box seating (a special section where you have luxury season seating). Because my friends knew I had some intuitive talent, they gave me $40 to place a bet on a horse. I bet on a longshot horse, which paid out $475 when it won its race. We all split the winnings.

On another occasion, my friend Denise took me to Las Vegas, where we walked around the casinos. She had me use my senses to pick a nickel gambling slot machine to play. We won $850.

As I gained a deeper awareness for my gifts, I came to feel that I should not take advantage of them; instead, I devoted myself to learning more about "intuitive gifts." In the course of my quest, I met many teachers, including Terry Cole-Whittaker, truly a frontrunner in the field; Rosalyn L. Bruyere; and Neale Donald Walsch – all of whom I found to be absolutely authentic and brilliant. I had a strong desire to maintain my connection to my higher self. I kept up my swimming, as part of this, just for the enjoyment of it.

One of the most memorable days of my life took place in Paris. I was a singer at the time and had done a tour in the musical *Grease*, then left Los Angeles after signing a recording contract with a company in Europe. It was my dream come true. I gave up my job, my home, and my car in the United States and moved to Paris.

But the recording deal fell through, due to personnel changes in the recording company, and I found myself in Paris without a job, a place to stay, or a way to cross the Atlantic and get back home. For three weeks, I wandered around the city, feeling frantic, desperate, and searching for a way to stay in Paris.

Intuitively, I went to Notre Dame Cathedral daily, searching for solace, praying as I had been taught. One Thursday, as I sat panicking in this glorious cathedral, on my knees in the wooden pew, my inner struggle became deafening. The hamster wheel of fear kept rolling around my head. I was resigned to the realities of returning to the States, with my dreams nothing but ash in the wind, and I thought this day might be my last goodbye.

I sat quietly, the hamster wheel finally stilled by feelings of sadness about saying farewell. My entire being was silent under the weight of saying goodbye to this stunning cathedral and its magnificent stained-glass windows.

I was still sitting in the corner, when all of a sudden, like a wave, this energy came toward me; it started to radiate a strong vibration and hovered over my head. I became frozen, transfixed in stillness. Suddenly, I felt the warmth of the sun on my shoulders. The rays were streaming in, spilling across the pews in front of me. The rays gave way to form, the shape of an angel, an entity that was joined by other angelic shapes, though only one of them communicated with me directly. I was overwhelmed by an overwhelming feeling of trust and calmness, and heard a voice inside tell me to remain in Paris, that there were lessons to learn, and that love would guide me.

"You are here to learn about us," this telepathic voice seemed to say.

"Who are you?" I asked.

"I am Archangel Michael," the voice said.

Inside my mind I responded, "I will do whatever it is you need me to do."

There was a strong feeling of agreement, and I felt a kind of blanket of love surround me, along with this comforting reassurance that everything was going to be more than all right.

I walked home along the banks of the River Seine in a kind of daze, wondering if that was a dream or if I had imagined the whole thing. The experience was so intense I wasn't sure what had transpired.

As I was walking in the door, the phone rang. It was a friend who worked for movie director Robert Altman. He was phoning to ask me to house sit for him in Montmartre, because he was returning to the United States to write a movie script. All I had to do was take care of his cat. Needless to say, the duration of my stay in Paris was filled with life-enriching lessons. It turned into a tremendous learning experience for me.

Like a miracle, the best possible outcome had come forth, and I was offered a place to live and afterward regained employment. I had a revelation, of which I will tell you more later.

Looking back, I'm so grateful for that detour into hardship in Paris, because it opened my heart to listening to divine guidance. As a result of that experience, I carry with me the knowledge that I am being guided by a higher power. I have continued to study and travel, sharing the lessons I've learned – and continue to learn, after my mind and heart learned to be receptive.

That year became another catalyst for me to immerse myself in the spiritual world. Having experienced amazing supernatural events in France, I had to open up to all realms of communication, past lives, and thoughts. I moved back to Los Angeles and continued to work in the entertainment field as a Hollywood talent manager and producer.

Hollywood has a way of keeping you on the edge of your seat, and to unwind I took up swimming again.

A few years later, while swimming in the USA Masters swimming division, I broke two world records in my age category, for the 100- and 200-meter backstroke. I discovered that I was rejuvenated in the realm of competition when I used my spiritual tools, and at the age of thirty-four, I found myself in deep: competing against fifteen- to twenty-three-year-olds (Janet Evans pre-Olympic 50 meter USC swim meet). Afterward, I retired from the competition aspect of the sport.

In time, and now well versed in my intuitive abilities, I was able to sense information about people when I would meet with them for work. Upon entering a studio or meeting prospective clients for the first time, I knew instantly whether the jobs were going to happen because of an initial feeling of connectivity – literally connecting me with numerous celebrities and powerful individuals in the entertainment limelight. Years of working with these individuals led me to become not only a talent manager but later a music and television producer as well.

After I had worked in the entertainment business for ten years, many of my friends encouraged me to channel my intuitive talents into a professional career by becoming an "intuitive life coach."

I was later persuaded by my clients to teach workshops and to write a book. Of course I said YES, and within three months my first book, *May the Angels Be with You*, was published by Random House. It became a best-seller, taking me to thirty-two U.S. cities and four countries on an extensive book tour.

One place I traveled was to London. After arriving at Heathrow Airport, I checked into the Royal Craven Hotel, where the bed felt how I imagined the bunks in maximum-security prison might feel. I awoke very early the next morning in order to make a 7 a.m. car pickup that was taking me to the ITV television studios. Random House had booked me on the top morning television chat show, *The Richard and Judy Show*, which is now called *This Morning*.

The hotel restaurant did not open for breakfast until 5:30 a.m., but I managed to find a Starbucks coffee shop on the Edgware Road. I walked along, thoughts of running into Mary Poppins in my mind, and absently hoped she would be able to fix my neck after a night on the lead hotel pillows. The caffeine helped me get back to the hotel to prepare for the day. Then the studio car picked me up, and I was whisked to the TV studios beside the River Thames.

Sarah Bennie, director of publicity for Random House, met me in the green room. Sarah is a great friend of mine – she feels like my long-lost sister, a person with great caring, who is also very down to earth. Being a Brit, her favorite word is "brilliant" – another word with excellent energy.

We were just discussing my upcoming Friday event when John, the events promoter, popped into the room. He said he was very worried, because he had only sold fifteen tickets and it was a nine-hundred-seat theater. I explained to them that there was no need to worry; we would fill up the venue by Friday. I shared with them my confidence that my activated intention, along with the power frequency of YES, would bring people to this venue. John's expression gave away that he was less than convinced, and I'm sure he thought I was a "certified delusional."

We sat in the green room, and within forty-five minutes, *The Richard and Judy Show* was transformed into an angelic heaven on an earthly stage, complete with two winged angel men who appeared in costumes.

I had no idea what to think – I just went along with the program. The producer escorted me onto the set, placing me next to Judy Finnigan and Richard Madeley. Judy spoke to me, but Richard ignored me. The studio lights went up, the television cameras' red lights were all turned on, and the countdown began. A voice over the intercom announced, "Action in five, four, three, two..." On "action," the director pointed, and the cameras came on, live on the air. The music punched as the cameras pushed in, and the show began.

The theme was "Learning to Access Your Angels," in conjunction with me giving personal cold readings to anyone they threw in front of me – in person or over the telephone.

As the show evolved, Judy would ask me questions about angels, and Richard would pull people from the audience and put them in front of me, saying "What are you getting on him or her?" – testing me as if I were some kind of trained seal. The more challenges they placed before me, the more I opened up to channeling the divine energy. Anything I said was downloaded from the truth. For every test they put before me, my answers were spot on – from the details of each person's individual situation to their names, and so on.

As the show progressed, Richard's mood shifted; he had now become my best friend, because he had become a believer, just like Judy. By the end of the show, they wanted photos with me and invited me to come back on the show again.

As I stepped out of the studio and into a cab back to the hotel, I was suddenly recognized. Every other person on the street was saying, "Hey, Angel Man, you were great." "We watched you this morning!" Sarah Bennie and I went to breakfast and then headed over to the BBC main western radio center to record fifteen segmented BBC Radio spots.

That afternoon, we did two newspaper and magazine interviews, had tea at Claridge's with the editor of *Vogue UK*, and did an *Instyle* magazine interview later that day. It was all quite miraculous! The evening ended with a wonderful fish dinner, and I didn't get back to the hotel until midnight.

As I headed to bed I looked out over the lights of nighttime London and thanked Archangel Michael for using me as a channel to help people, thereby offering me all of these wondrous opportunities.

The following morning we were off to Manchester to appear on two more television shows and do an interview at Granada ITV Studios, where the longest-running soap opera in the UK, *Coronation Street*, and many other productions took place.

As the days passed and Friday's event got closer, the press I was receiving built and built, and by Friday a plethora of people were there to attend my evening event. I think my favorite moment was John absolutely beaming when he came into the room and announcing that we'd sold 799 seats.

From London, I headed back to the United States, to New York City, continuing the tour through thirty-seven cities. My professional life-coaching calendar was overflowing. The YES Frequency and its formula for successful living worked its wonders in the lives of my clients. It is my privilege and joy to share it with you. In life there are many beginnings, and this is a wonderful technique to help you find your way.

YES, I carry this light within me at all times.

Sharing positive notions and actions is the light that will bring and give everlasting gifts. Your entire nature will light the way for a better existence – not just for yourself but for all you encounter. You will become the light you are looking for.

Core YES Codes

The Core YES Codes are the foundation on which you will build your personal mission statement – a key part of what makes The YES Frequency so effective. They will help you clarify your focus for your mission statement. Think of it as uncovering your personal code of honor by reaching way down deep within and prioritizing your values and beliefs. This exploration of ethics is necessary in order to build a straightforward and powerful understanding of your goals, which is always the first step in reaching them.

When your thoughts are sparked by positive thinking and uphold your inner values, this creates an invisible intention that will dictate your future. Your values cradle your destiny.

Every human being has a hierarchy of principles. Much of this has its origins in your upbringing. And these thoughts generate patterns of thinking and lay out how you see your life. As you prioritize your higher ethics, and as you choose to do this exploration of your deep values and beliefs, you are creating a habit or code that links you to the pattern you want to live by.

Core YES Codes include all that you love doing. Make a list. For example, if you are great at giving advice and fixing everyone else's problems, include that. Unless you are a counselor, or some other profession that focuses on caring for other people, fixing everyone else's problems means you are undoubtedly taking a back seat in your own life. Focus on yourself, and get clear about what you want. If you are unsatisfied with where your life is, begin to drive your thoughts to the destination where you want to be living. It is imperative that you envision living in this feeling of what it would feel like to arrive at your actual "dream" destination. This Core YES Code will push you to place yourself in the driver's seat of your own life.

For example, I had a client who loved music and was passionate about opera music. While she was growing up, being an opera singer was her dream and her priority. But as my client examined this dream, she found it to be untenable. Through the many trials and tribulations of auditioning, it became apparent that her voice was not a strong enough instrument to achieve this particular goal.

But through the power of living within The YES Frequency, she chose to be positive about her life in spite of the obstacles. She continued to immerse herself in the opera community. She volunteered to cover certain opera events, helped with handing out programs at the New York Metropolitan Opera, and developed her skills in selling tickets and becoming an advocate for the subscription list. All of these initiatives kept her close to these same like-minded people who loved the same things she did.

While working at these events, she met a prominent operetta talent agent; eventually, because of her expertise in knowing the opera singers and the stories of the operas, an opportunity revealed itself, when she got into a conversation with the agent and revealed that she knew everyone on their talent list.

The agent was so impressed with her knowledge of opera, and so taken with the fact that she knew his client list, he hired her as his assistant. Now she works at a top-notch agency representing some of the most astonishing opera talent. She gets to travel the world, and better, her dedication to her love of opera has created a fulfilling life path for her, immersed in the power of YES.

Her priority of music and opera was on her Core YES Code list, and she did something about it. Even when she was rejected, she forged ahead and innovated to keep her dream close to her heart. Is it any wonder that her dream came true? She is no longer floating from one unfulfilling job to another.

The concerted effort my client made to align directly with the frequency and prioritize her attachment to her dream by keeping it at the top of her list is what allowed it to come to fruition. Her ability to stay focused, positive, and clear in her mission placed her right in the center of the magical frequency of YES, because her vision and balanced values never faltered.

Core YES Codes will become your personal statement of how to tap into your frequency. They serve as your own personal recipe of listed values, including those involved in building your vision. All strategies that will ultimately connect The YES Frequency begin by customizing your own Core YES Codes.

First, you need to find your values (remember that these are not just abstract concepts; they can be as individual as a deep love for opera). Shortly, we will do an exercise to write these values down and refine them, but for now, just set your mind on following this process. Remember that defining your personal Core YES Code is the pathway to clarity for your mission statement.

Additional Core YES Codes

Yes, I'm on it! (Procrastinate no more)

– Leap into the positive notion of joy, and surrender all negativity. When you allow yourself to live inside that joy, everything and everyone around you will feel the frequency of YES.

Yes, I can! (Stop the excuses for why you can't do it)

– When you truly believe that "YES, you can," all the excuses that have hampered you in the past disintegrate. Moreover, they become completely unimportant because you are focusing on the motion of positive energy.

Yes, I am! (Erase the thoughts of "If only...")

– Now you are letting go of all the "if only" thoughts that never served your initiative anyway! Living inside the frequency of "YES, I am" is like living inside the feeling of a glowing suntan.

Yes, I have! (Change feelings of "lacking" to gratitude)

– You will reside inside this purification frequency of feeling good about yourself! As you are! Right inside this moment of complete acceptance! You will carry it forward and into every part of your being. This momentum of "Yes, I am" will overpower all insecurity.

Yes, I will! (Push through and let go of those who have said NO)

Life Key Code

You cannot be true to yourself unless you activate and unlock who you are and what it is you truly want.

Core YES Code

Summary exercises to assist in honing in on your goal.

After you write down everything that you love to do, this next exercise will help you define your core values. Take a moment and really define your valued want. Is your highest value to save money to buy a home? Is your highest value to find a fulfilling partner? Maybe a new job that you love? Or do you want to be a curator for a modern museum?

When you are aligned to your higher values you become inspired. In order to visualize your dreams, you first have to visualize and list the higher values that make that dream so important to you. Because if there's something you don't love doing, it should not be on your priority list.

Simple Core YES Code Strategies

> When exclaiming the following, be clear and concise. This will feed your dreams and help your goals to manifest.

When you align to your higher values, you become inspired. When you are in alliance with love, you become successful and focused with purpose. Decide what your higher values are – meaning, if your higher priority is family coming first, or if you are someone who places their spirituality first. When you are hiring someone, find out what his or her highest value is in their life. It will tell you so much about this person.

Most important, though, finding your highest value will tell you what you need to know about yourself. In this next exercise, be succinct, honest, and true to your authentic self.

First, build a list of your values:

Next, write down everything that you that you love to do:

_____

_____

_____

_____

_____

Write the names of people who spiritually make a difference to you

_____

_____

_____

_____

_____

Who are your heroes?

_____

_____

_____

_____

_____

Make a list of what really gives you inspiration:

_____

_____

_____

_____

_____

Clearly state and prioritize your wants:

_____

_____

_____

_____

_____

How are you using the time you have to work toward these values?

_____

_____

_____

_____

_____

Write down your favorite motivational phrases:

_____

_____

_____

_____

_____

Who would you really love to meet and work with?

_____

_____

_____

_____

_____

Write down your favorite inspirational quotes, especially those by people you admire:

_____

_____

_____

_____

_____

Think about the values you have written above, along with the people who inspire you and the desires you want to move toward in a fulfilling life. All of these values and priorities should give you some idea of the life path you want to follow to be in tune with The YES Frequency. Remember that your Core YES Code is the foundation for your mission statement. Now thinking about all of this, write your personal Core Code:

_____

_____

_____

_____

_____

Identifying Your Goals

Now that you have your Core Code, the next step is to take it and specifically identify your goals in the order you want to make them happen. This will help you paint the picture in your mind, coloring your everyday thought process to activate your frequency for success. This is what is needed to get inside The

YES Frequency. Liken this in your mind to the laws of attraction: even when we do not understand attraction, the pull is there, and identifying your goals will help pull you into The YES Frequency in this same way.

Envision yourself completely prepared, sitting at the desk of the business you want to run, or see yourself at the helm of the publishing company you dream of leading as editor-in-chief. If you need more tangible tools, make a clear, definitive vision board with the steps to your goals written alongside your Core Code. Be aware that if you do not define your life, someone will define it for you.

In your everyday life, communicate about values with the people who are in your trajectory via work, relationships, family, and friends. Through conversation, gently explore what their values are. How do you react to them and how they value themselves and others? Knowing more about the people you are confronted with helps you to decipher healthy intentions.

Through the years, your highest values will probably change. When we are young, many times our highest values are to have freedom, buy a car, see the world, or finish school.

Some of us choose a value that is out of balance with our true selves for our "highest value"; people who do this can be pulled off track for years. I have seen endless cases like this.

One of my clients had decided that her highest value was money. Her thought process involved financial security, and her idea of success was to be surrounded by celebrity. I tried to implement a different philosophy of success, but she would not be deterred. A luxurious life and red carpets were the only things she understood as achievement. She surrounded herself with like-minded people with superficial "wants," and she was convinced that only these physical manifestations of financial success would bring her happiness. She would say things like, "Show me the man's friends, and I will show you the man" and twist the meaning in a way that serviced her "wants." Slowly, she cut herself off from everyone who didn't have enough money to go to her five-star restaurants, parties, and vacation spots. She married a man who was well off and accomplished her "want," and as time passed she and I lost touch.

Six years later we ran into one another in an airport lounge. When she called my name, I barely recognized her. I asked her if she was happy. Her expression gave her away.

Through her story, I learned that the priority of "superficial value" in life led her to a place of uncertainty about who her friends really were. She suddenly found herself living a kind of reality show–styled life. Her friendships were really just acquaintances with jet-set people who thought just like her, and who weren't really interested in anything but being entertained and spending money. Now that she was older, she was not being included in the A list jet-set clan. She found herself rejected, and surrendered to the fever of addiction to plastic surgery in hopes of recapturing the earlier glory days. I did not hear any of this from her directly – it was simply in the subtext of her words and all over her face. Happiness? Not so much. You have heard the expression: "Be careful what you wish for – you just might get it."

I wish I could say she has changed and found happiness, but in her process of peeling back the layers of the onion she has unfortunately gone to even more profound lengths of superficiality and dug herself into a space where she feels her money kept her from hitting bottom. This is interesting to me, because I feel hardships would have taught her humility, compassion, and more. Losing her money might have been the only thing that could have saved her.

In my second book, *Living in the Spiritual Zone*, I refer to having found that, just like in a twelve-step program, if a person does not hit a kind of bottom, they don't know how to rebuild their lives. If your values are askew, it will defer your spiritual success. Many billionaires are miserable because of just this truth. Figuring out and acting in alignment with your core values is integral.

Bring to mind the company you keep. What are your friends and associates like? What are their values? How is associating with those people and their beliefs affecting your life? How do they treat other people in their lives, including the ones who only pass through? Pay attention to the behavior of people in your life, and it will reveal a great deal about their character.

Many people will take on the "victim" mentality and become used to that whining style of living wherein the glass is half-empty. In this way, they become one-sided and not in the flow with the universe.

You must learn to communicate by becoming effective. Being a top seller in any field is about learning how to communicate. If you are full of enthusiasm and positivity, you will magnetize opportunities and great people toward you. Create the events that inspire you, and you will inspire others to join your cause, and, in this case, help you to build your mission statement.

Being in alignment with your MISSION is essential to CUSTOMIZING YOUR DREAMS and achieving RESULTS.

Formulating Your Mission Statement

When you create a mission statement you are branding yourself, the same way that a logo brands a product. You are activating a blueprint that goes into the universe. When you create this blueprint, it actually goes into your subconscious mind and works toward activating the path for you. To achieve your desires, follow The YES Frequency; it will act as a tool to give you the unlimited results you want to live in and by.

Make the program for your brain. Just as you would program your computer with your favorite files on your desktop, you use this same kind of software application for your brain. This is in order to activate your YES Frequency, placing you into action with respect to your values.

Create a focal point as a kind of final destination. For example, if you are trying to complete a book or build a company, or if you want to be an actor, you should be placing your Core Code deciding factors on a list. Think of it as packing your suitcase.

Step 1

Write down several activities that you love. Look for things that are easy for you – things that you may not have received any training in, but nonetheless they just come naturally to you.

I love to

_____

Step 2

Write down a few top qualities that you love about yourself or that others have seen in you or complimented you on. What are your talents and strengths? Please do not be modest about your best talents. Be positive about the places you are already strong.

I am proud to be

_____

Step 3

Write down the qualities that you would like to possess/achieve.

I would like to be

_____

Step 4

Synthesize your steps in order of your priorities.

Finally, it's time to take all the talents/elements outlined above and formulate your mission statement toward your goals, utilizing all these steps and combining everything you've uncovered into one strong mission statement.

Imagine a timeline that records every key experience of your life until this point. Notice events and activities that created a special feeling for you when they happened – things that you feel you would like to do more often.

What is your fantasy *ideal* day? This is not a vacation day, but rather envision an ideal day that is still the midst of responsibilities and includes involvement with other people. Include events and activities that are especially meaningful to you.

How can your talents and abilities work together? Each one of us lives in the context and environment of others' abilities, which color and shape all of our lives. How can these talents come together in harmony to fulfill your mission statement? The combination of these three steps create the goal for your life and is the foundation for your mission statement.

If you were a company, how would you want to be branded? What kind of logo, theme song, or title would you choose? What would you like to have? Be? Create? It could be a new job, more money, a new relationship. It could be becoming more spiritually sound. State very simply exactly what you would like to do in this lifetime. This will identify and hone your purpose.

Each and every thought will advance your mission statement. Really own the energy of the words you use. Words are very simple, but they have great power. Let's use an example.

Think of the word "confidence." What is confidence to you? What about joy? What about love? What about really trying to see what we can become rather than simply trying to manifest more money? Granted, all of us could use more money. But let's change the energy first. Let's pick the energy of confidence. How would you like to manifest as a confident person? In your mission statement, let's make confidence step 1. Now think about step 2. What would you like to create? Would it be a new job?

As an example, let's say you want a new job in marketing. Let's say you are working for a company, but you want to market yourself in a new career working in high-tech products, such as computers, advertising, or being a copywriter. For now, let's just make the mission statement and put the words together. If you need to reach for a pen and paper, go ahead and do so.

Let's start with this:

I have an incredible new job working in the high-tech world.

Remember, this isn't just about a job. You can apply this to anything in your life – it's your vision. As you have your vision of that mission statement, think about how you would really feel if you had that job right now?

When identifying your goals and building your mission statement, "want" is subjective. When deciding on your goals, be straightforward and clear. Be the audience of your life and validate the positive character within you. Believe that you can advance and make that advancement a priority. When watching a movie, you pick who you want to win in a story. Or when you read a book, you get attached to a particular character because of their values – or, for entertainment's sake, their lack of values. However, in order to become the hero or heroine of your own life, you need to make the choices that validate your character's journey. In doing so you need to create a clear-cut mission statement – meaning, when you take action, create events or situations that are in alignment to your highest values. This will help you become motivated and inspired to follow through with commitments that are in alignment with your values. When all these things are in harmony, you are able to become focused and successful in bringing your future dream into the present moment.

In part, your mission statement is a private matter. It is important to only tell people who have the same mindset as you about your mission statement – those who support you, who are spiritually sound, who are willing to align with those thoughts, and want the highest good for you. Make a note of those who don't believe in following your heart or dreams; in most cases, you will find it is simply because they didn't continue following theirs.

As this mission statement is strictly for you, you should write or speak about your personal mission statement as if it is already true. For example, someone in the field of real estate might have as their mission statement: "I'm a multibillion-dollar real estate agent and a conduit to endless opportunities." When you take action through a complete commitment to believing it is, receiving becomes abundant. This is not lying to yourself; it is establishing a clear line of thinking and speaking of the word, so that you preach it as an end result, and in this way bring it about.

This is not going on your résumé, so jump in – it's okay, it's *your* mission.

I remember traveling to New York City to meet different book publishers and telling myself, "I'm not coming home without a publisher and a book deal." That was possible because I had done the research and had a mission statement that was in balance with my vibrations experience. It is helpful to be balanced about how you house your mission statement.

It's important that your mission statement be life-affirming for you and work toward the highest goals you identified, and aligned with the rest of your life. Imagine if you created a mission statement that was outlandish and stated something like, "I want to buy NASA and reignite the space program." Unless you are Sir Richard Branson (an English business magnate and owner of Virgin Records and Virgin Airlines), you are not being pragmatic. If you were a billionaire who had lost money, you would already have that understanding of living in that vibration and energy.

Again, if you have been a wealthy entrepreneur already, you will attract that likeness because your vibration is already in alignment and at that level. If you are coming from scarcity, or lack consciousness and have a limited belief system, you must change that and work through the steps before you can write something that you can attain.

Part of that is changing the old ways of thinking by repeating your positive mission statement. The subconscious mind is similar to a sponge: it soaks up everything and holds onto it; it makes a Xerox or blueprint of everything we have seen or done or witnessed. The body doesn't lie. If you speak endlessly about how ill you are or joke about being sick, eventually you can become sick based on your subconscious and how it activates thoughts into feelings. If you say you are sick for six weeks, your body won't know any better and you will become sick. If you keep repeating that, you will create that mantra somewhere in your life. You will manifest that in your body, around you, or somewhere else in your life, even if you should be perfectly healthy.

Therefore, it is important that you choose your thoughts and words carefully. When tying these Core Codes together (your values, vision, and strategies) into your mission statement, you will embody The YES Frequency. State it to the universe as a declaration for you to manifest the end result. This kind of declaration synchronizes us, and puts us in alignment with our true hearts' desires.

Which may be said as:

I am an incredible_____ traveling the world.

My work as a_____ affords me endless choices.

My relationship brings_____ and is full of love and support.

My job has opened_____, giving me the chance to buy my new_____.

My art is now valued_____, creating my own_____.

I am involved with the_____ ,and my philanthropy has_____.

Every year I travel to_____ and make a difference.

I am a successful, world-class_____ , helping to change the world.

I attract a wonderful_____ , and I have loving relationships.

I am healed in all aspects_____ and am at peace; life is joyful.

I'm a well-respected _____ , and I am healing people.

You can have many subtexts within your mission statement, or list them in terms of priority. You may decide you need more than one. Whatever works for you and complements your grand plan is how you should delineate your list. Again, please try to choose mission statements that are pragmatic, and therefore attainable. With the frequency matching your vibration, you can attain the results you want. When you are confident in this practice, you are training your subconscious to live in a higher vibration. With that, your mission statement can become attainable.

But you must be diligent and do your work. By this, I'm merely suggesting that it is not a good idea to spend your time unwisely. For example, if you are in your eighties and you want to be an athlete in the Olympics, you may find you need to transform this dream using The YES Frequency: you may be better able to experience the energy and joy you seek by purchasing a ticket to the Olympics, instead. Or, thinking about your highest values might reveal that rather than being in the Olympics specifically, your true dream is recognition of your physical prowess, or proving to yourself that this strength is still within you. Be the first octogenarian to finish a local walking marathon. Consider the heart of your Core Code, instead of letting the word NO rise from within you to interfere with your vibrations.

If you want to be a world-class author you must have some knowledge of your subject, or be willing to dive deep into the work and learn the whole process of what it takes to write a book. This will guide you through the steps that you need to take to back up your mission statement. Your mission statement is almost like a marketing strategy for how you want to see your future.

The exercise below will reinforce this understanding. It is a kind of confirmation of how you would feel living in "success mode." When you assemble the whole recipe, you immediately step into the frequency.

Exercise

Take some time and write down or speak with your partner about what your dream would look like. Where would you be living? Who would you be with? How would you speak? What would be your life's work? What kind of people would you associate with? And ultimately, how would you feel in the midst of all this success?

By telling your story as you want it to go and placing it in the present tense, you will alter your chronicle of the future in all areas and bring it forward.

Here's an example to follow:

> I have a beautiful home in Los Angeles. I'm traveling the world painting, and my work is being exhibited by the top museums. I am supported by a loving partner who is positive and also pursuing their ultimate successful life. I associate with people whose highest values are in harmony with mine, and I feel surrounded by positivity and energized to fulfill my dreams.

In any way, shape, or form, express your vision of how you want to be living your life, and work especially hard to feel the "as if" of what it would feel like to live inside the feeling mode of success.

Here are some of the places the success mode might lead you:

- Having an office or a studio.

- Offering consultations for my _____ project.

- Bring assistance to my travel plans.

- Planning dates for seminars in other countries.

- Making audio CDs for distribution.

- Recording or performing over the globe.

- Having lunch with _____ and the
  Dalai Lama.

Take steps 1–4 and write a long-form practice draft of your mission statement. Don't worry about the length – just quickly write a version that you can use now, then consolidate your mission statement later.

While you are building and attaining these kinds of mission statements, keep in mind the trajectory to your goal. If you have no prior spiritual experience or connection to the possibility of meeting the Dalai Lama, it's still possible that you may meet him in passing, but in order to have a real exchange you must be on the path of that vibration to actually attain your mission statement. By this I mean, it's important to be well read in the subjects you want to participate in.

I had years of experience working within the entertainment community. Working with these various celebrities meant that it was a vibrational energy that I was in, and a frequency I was comfortable with and used to. For example, I had seen the film *Life is Beautiful*; I had a deep respect for the message the film portrayed and how it was a great metaphorical teacher in how to rise above and strive to create love and beauty, even in the most terrifying, dark, and desperate of situations. It also provided an example of what superlative parenting could achieve. I wanted to say thank you to the director of the film. So for me to say, "I will be meeting Roberto Benigni and giving him a private session" was in the realm of my vibrations, and therefore attainable to me. Even though I did not in fact know him personally, I had already been around the frequency of many people in the public eye who worked in the entertainment field, so I already had a sense of what that would feel like.

Naturally, if I had some notion of wanting to work for the United Nations and no educational understanding of what that entailed, it would be rather futile, as I would have no vibrations that allowed me to understand what that energy is all about – never mind the language skills and geographical understanding required.

Some people, much like children, are wooed by job titles that are just superficial "wants," such as, ballet dancer, president, actor, model, architect, executive producer, director, or banker, without doing or understanding the educational research and actual dedicated, trained, hands-on work and building a résumé toward that purpose. Again, the superficial want of the title alone is without meaning. Head-in-the-clouds wants without due diligence will make your path a long walk through sand dunes, and your dreams will be like a mirage in the distance, rather than a real, achievable destination.

So you really have to choose mission statements that are conscientious about the vibrations you are comfortable in. Naturally, most anything is attainable with education and persistence and hard work, but don't expect that anything will just arrive at your front door. Pick one mission statement to be your first goal, work toward that until you achieve it, then pick a higher goal and create a new mission statement. Continue reaching higher and higher, so that you are moving in the right direction of elevating your goals. Every time you reach your goal, you say, "Okay, I can check off that mission statement," and you move on.

For each new mission statement, you can add new elements, and any big goal might have any number of mission statements within it. You do have to keep feeding your emotional state of mind, which means that you want to think right, get proper rest, exercise, and eat organically/healthily. Without maintaining the emotional state of mind, it is very difficult to reach that frequency. So really take stock of what it is that you are saying, eating, breathing, thinking. Because what you are thinking, you will develop into, and what you are eating you will become, what you say will become what you do, and everything encompasses what you grow to be. Please be aware that you are a part of the cause and effect, which is a domino effect.

It may not hit today, but quite possibly next week or six months from now that the things you have been thinking and saying will put that into motion. When you become really clear and good at this, you will attract The YES Frequency instantly.

To return to the example from my own life: Upon attracting the encounter with Roberto Benigni, I was gratified that it was quite wondrous. Roberto is an extraordinary, kind, and gifted man. Six months after our meeting he won Best Actor and Best Foreign Film for *Life is Beautiful* at the Academy Awards.

I later attracted my first book deal by creating the right energy frequency, wherein the manifestation occurred within a few months. When I wanted to go to Japan, it manifested in six months. Italy took patience and commitment, but three years later I was there. In the meantime, I was working on my mission statement, going so far as listening to Italian language and music CDs and eating pasta. When I finally achieved this mission statement, I not only traveled to Italy but now I return every year, and I feel very at home there.

This is what I envisioned it would feel like to be in these countries, accompanied by a progression of attaining my valued wants, one step at a time.

Taking action is essential. I had an ongoing mission statement that I kept actively feeding, until eventually it became a reality. Now I teach it all over the world. When you follow this formula, your frequency thrives by adding all those components to the work "behind the scenes," so to speak, of your mission statement. You are producing your own movie, in a sense. Produce your life the way you want to see it. Your frequency goes up by getting it to a level where you will manifest it, drawing these events to you because you actually have visualized them.

You must choose things that you can attain. If you are already an actor, then it is feasible that you may have the opportunity to work with your favorite actor someday. When creating your statement, if you have the basis of criteria, you may have an undercurrent of The YES Frequency in the body of your statement, meaning that you may carry the feeling that it is happening right now. So in your mission statement, you may write your "as if" and say to yourself: "I will be filming a movie opposite Meryl Streep and playing as her friend, sibling, or some such." That is plausible if your vibration is already hovering in that arena. If not, you need to take steps to get in the trajectory of the destination you want to reach, or readjust your statement.

Please be reasonable in your thought process. If you are somewhere in Boston, and you are working in a bowling alley, on a golf course, or for the Queen's Guard and nowhere near a film school, and you are *not* studying or volunteering at a theater, taking a film class, or studying film history online, a mission statement about acting alongside Meryl Streep is not going to happen quickly. You have to start by getting yourself to that frequency level. So you really need to move in that vibration, and take the necessary steps to get closer to it. You have to work at it every day – not part time or every other day or on weekends. Every time I do a seminar, it is constant retraining, feeding the mind until it changes.

If your subconscious is saturated in YES, you can eventually turn YES into a reality, and then you will attract all these beautiful events and people into your frequency.

Create Your Own Private Mission Statement

If you are surrounded by people who express strong opposition to your dreams, only share your mission statement with those whom you trust, people who believe in and support you. Those who love you may not understand, so it may be helpful to protect your mission statement. There are too many negative people who are more than willing to shoot you down. Do yourself a favor and avoid that unnecessary negative blockage.

Many people are projecting their own fear upon you with

"no way" thoughts, more of which I know I don't need to spell out. You can practice the language of positive speaking, or the language of miracles – it's really just about learning how to frame the words away from NO and into YES, and always reaching for possibility. Envision framing your emotional home and building your dream home with no obstacles, facing confrontation without fear.

This doesn't mean that if you nap continually that your dreams will manifest your goals. But if you carry the idea of YES with you as you evolve daily toward your destination, you will arrive.

This living "as if" delivers an undercurrent that adds to the momentum of your goal: believing in yourself and moving forward as if it actually is in motion. "Living as if" is a positive investment in reaching your goal.

Defining "living as if" means selectively choosing your words to evoke the positive results you want: "My dream is to travel the world with my job," and so on. This is something that you would like to happen. This doesn't bend the truth in any way. It wouldn't be helpful to your goals to have someone exclaim that you are not living in the truth. That said, they can't do anything to stop you from thinking it as such. Refine your ideals to verbiage of positive truths. It is a matter of choosing your vernacular carefully. So when I say living "as if," I don't mean for you to alter your reality and live inside falsehoods, but that you should alter your state of mind to think about and envision your perspective of unlimited powers within The YES Frequency.

Let's say your dream is to buy a home in the country. And yes, I encourage you to live "as if." That said, it isn't helpful to lie and tell people, "I have a house in the country." But I encourage you to think about and envision that home. And when you speak of it, you should say, "I see myself owning a house in the country." If you want to attain a particular cherished position at work, for example, again keeping the "as if" in motion, you should say, "I relish the thought of one day taking ownership."

I want to mention, though, that this concept of living "as if" is completely different when it comes to personal health. For the betterment of individuals' welfare, it is absolutely critical that we believe, envision, and state it as such:

"YES, I will get better."

"YES, I'm feeling better every day."

"YES, I am getting stronger every day."

This type of YES affirmation is not only beneficial but critical to healing. Affirmative thinking and speaking is imperative in rehabilitation of any kind. One must reach into that powerful positive healing frequency. In many instances, when doctors have given a patient a diagnosis, they have told the patient of certain negative results or restrictions they will face, but through sheer persistence and mind over matter, positive thinking, and endless perseverance, the patient rises above these restrictions. There are endless stories of people who have overcome adversity and lived no doubt differently from before but not without choices about their life and destination.

With your mission statement in place, you are now ready to get on that plane and fly to your destination.

Considering the steps from your Core Code highest values, build onto and carry over steps 1–4 and consolidate your mission statement here.

_____

_____

_____

_____

The Application of the Sun

If you do not plant positive thoughts in your mind, your garden of greatness will not grow, never mind flourish.

The temperature of the sun is so powerful it radiates nearly 93 million miles (150 million km) away from Earth, far enough for light generated there to take over eight minutes to reach us. The sun is responsible for the bounty of life on our planet; flowers open beneath it, and birds bask in its warmth. The sun is the life force of everything on Earth. It may even be thought of as the brainpower of the Earth, for without it, the world as we know it would not exist.

We must learn to replace old patterns and create new ones, using the sun as a reminder to embrace success and happiness. The shift must take place internally. If you would like to create something different, you must do something different. The following technique is designed to create change.

Sun and Warmth is my most powerful technique for finding your center when things in your life may be feeling out of tilt. In the following section, paint a picture in your mind as you read these words:

Think back to a time, some chilly day, when you recall that first feeling of stepping out of the cool shade and moving forward into the gentle, warm sun. What is the first thing you say when you feel that transition of coolness to the rays of sun, radiating like a comfortable blanket all over and warming your chilled body?

"Ahhhh, yes!"

It is the same feeling when you step inside a warm shower.

"Ahhhh, yes!"

Imagine yourself on the earth's stage in a beautiful garden, on a beach, or at the top of a mountain, with the sun warming your body. It's the same feeling you get when you are chilled and then step into the warm water of a morning bath. That calming exclamation...

"Ahhhh, yes."

As you sink into the tub, and allow the water to make you feel weightless as it soaks into your body, it also gives you that same feeling of pure acceptance in the moment before you begin the work of washing:

"Ahhhh, yes."

This feeling is what I want you to lean on and go to in times of challenge. When you are facing uncomfortable confrontations, arm yourself with this feeling. In practice, I want to build your sense memory of this positive feeling, so that you can more easily bring it with you when you are faced with adversity.

No matter what your station in life, we all know this universal feeling – we have all felt it at one time or another in our lives. So please sit down in your favorite place, real or in your mind's memory. Just find it!

Is it in your best friend's backyard by the pool, where you played when you were ten? Or maybe simply break time at work, when you sit by the heater in the hallway? Is it a memory from a vacation in Hawaii, relaxing under a palm tree on the beach? Or is it someplace you have seen in a magazine: the ocean cliffs off the coast of Spain? Is it a memory of the sun's warmth, or of a sulfur spa in Luxembourg? In the desert, a church, a lake, a forest? Or is it the memory of a scene from your favorite movie? Maybe that day when you slipped your feet beneath the warm sand by the river's edge.

Use your reality or your imagination and go to your own island of warmth in the sun in your mind. Wear the colors that make you feel beautiful, or better yet lay down in your God-given birthday suit and allow your skin to drink in the rays of the sun and that feeling of YES!

Lay back as that feeling warms your being; as the sun overtakes you, envision what you want. See yourself in that purpose of the experience. Say YES to that feeling of "being there" or "accomplishment" or "completion" or "the finish line," or whatever it is you are heading for.

Just be there now in that YES feeling of warmth and allow it to coat your being! Especially in times of turbulence in your life or when faced with opposition, step inside that feeling before you react. I guarantee it will be easier to deal with any problems you face if you are coming from that place.

As you face your first day with this new awareness of the sun, take with you this feeling of peace. When you live in an embodiment of love, forgiveness, and permission to speak truths, you will create an amazing life. Self-love has nothing to do with using yourself as an object; it means that you love and respect yourself from within. I promise that your relationships with others will change dramatically as you change yourself and access the self-love within.

Core Life Codes

The quality of your thoughts determines the quality of your life. There are laws and principles for us to follow, and if we desire to flourish and fulfill our potential we must be willing to accept the good parts of ourselves, as well as the adverse parts.

2

The Forgiving Frequency

Life Key Code

Forgive those who have broken your faith in you, and moreover forgive yourself. Forgiving yourself and all others is integral to your future success.

If you are not able to manifest things, or if you get angry and give up and raise the same list of excuses and blame – take note, this will stop you moving forward in your life. When you validate why you can't have what you want, this creates a cycle of thinking in which you're stuck like a hamster going around on an exercise wheel. This keeps you grounded. You will not be able to fly and enter The YES Frequency.

Over the years many negative things have no doubt happened to you. If you have survived a breakup or a betrayal, a fight with someone, or a disappointing work situation, blame is one part of so many things that you could be hanging on to. But in order to make space for the subconscious to activate the frequency for your dreams and wishes, and to make room for positivity in your life, you must let go of the past weight that has stayed with you from all of these situations or events. This is called the power of forgiveness.

You need to think about the endless barriers that you are throwing up, which stop you from realizing your dreams. Through positive repetition you can break your negative cycles, but the only way to have a proper breakthrough is to eradicate the old behavior that is blocking you.

You need to change the direction from which you are approaching your wants in life. In order for you to break the pattern of negatives, you may need to give extra attention to your past and finding forgiveness. Because when you are holding negative energy from people or situations inside your cellular level, you are holding the memory in your subconscious and your conscious mind. This means you are *not* running the show in your life. The events and situations from your past will take over and control your future actions. Forgiveness is about decoding these blocked or stuck energies.

Below is the key phrase that will target these blocked energies. Please take the time to repeat each line with conviction. Repetition is what allows the healing to take place:

"I forgive myself and all others."

"I forgive myself and all others."

"I forgive myself and all others."

"I forgive myself and all others."

Taking Responsibility

By taking responsibility for your emotions, or the "negative side of your story," you will face a kind of "truth mirror" – the truth being, to what degree did your stance of not forgiving work for you? Think about it. Is it possible, in your life before today, that you gained something from choosing not to forgive? Your instant reaction will be to fight me on this, but just hear me out for a minute.

Sometimes we choose not to forgive because we perceive the

act of forgiving as the equivalent of saying "It's okay" to whatever transpired. That is *not* what I am saying at all. After we've been wronged in some way, or we've done something wrong, the last thing we usually want to do is lift the burden by labeling the act or situation as okay.

Forgiveness isn't about justifying someone else's actions. It isn't for them at all. It is for YOU!

It's not about freeing someone of his or her guilt or telling someone that everything's all right now. It's about letting go with love, not clinging to the anger as a form of identity. What you have survived as an individual is turbulent, to say the least, but you cannot move yourself forward by being driven by the anger of the past.

There are a plethora of reasons why you might want to continue to express the anger, rage, or whining disappointments of what could have been, or of how dare they! Understand that the only person you are punishing with this ranting verbiage is yourself; it is destroying your positive frequency in life.

The exclamations are varied and endless. Some of the instances of being wronged are profound and life-threatening. Oddly, I have found that the victims in those cases are sometimes the first people to forgive. I think the idea that their life was spared gives them a feeling of "I am grateful to be alive" instead of focusing on the anger or unfairness.

Another perceived motivation for choosing not to forgive is that we feel so desperately hurt; we convince ourselves that as

> *"Forgiveness is an act of LOVE. It is through humility and realism that you are now coming to remember that you deserve the gift of forgiveness – forgiving others and forgiving yourself.*
> *It is one of the ultimate acts of self-love because it will bring you back to yourself. Holding onto anger and resentment costs you. In reality, the person you punish when you hold onto anger and resentment is yourself. Forgiveness sets you free."*
>
> Gary Quinn

long as we stay angry, we will remember what happened to us and warn those around us – that if we stay angry, we will never go through this again. Sometimes it's just a case of feeling abandoned. So the intent is, through defamation of character, you are trying to force people to take your side. Naturally, this is often about being angry due to hurt feelings. You might use indignation and anger as a shield, a self-defense mechanism. But that shield is what prevents you from receiving the opportunity to live in joy.

In rare cases, an actual horrific injustice has occurred, and the individual feels if they forgive the perpetrator, that would be unconscionable to the person who was victimized. Some cases require different levels of understanding. Even with that clarified, it is still better for your soul to forgive inside. This doesn't need to be a grand statement – just do it for yourself. Our fear is that, should we ever completely forgive, our wall of protection will crumble, leaving us emotionally raw. The truth is, we are always vulnerable. As human beings with emotions, we are susceptible. But that same susceptibility is also what allows us to experience happiness, joy, and all the other uplifting emotions.

The barriers we put up when we choose not to forgive can't really protect us from getting hurt again. It's an illusion. In truth, fighting to maintain our hurt only perpetuates the pain. It's by breaking that pattern that you put an end to the negative feelings. When you forgive, that wall comes down – and with it, all of the baggage you've been carrying around that stems from old anger and resentment. Try and understand: we have NO control over other people. We can't *make* them sorry. There is no objective gauge we can use that tells us, "Okay, *now* they are truly sorry; *now* they deserve to be forgiven."

The reason forgiveness is one of the ultimate acts of self-love is because it removes the need and pressure for you to be "The Judge." In some instances, certain people feel powerful in the judgment seat; they like presiding over the facts and exclaiming how good they are when those who wronged them are so very bad. They make themselves out to be the protagonist of the drama. Many thrive on repeating that same monologue again and again. Being the Judge makes them feel they are in control of the situation. Honestly, it is a lonely place to be.

For those of you who have had situations that separated you from your family, friends, and colleagues, or the relationships you were in became so vitriolic and condemning that you slammed a door that you now wish were slightly ajar, but you are stuck out in the cold due to your grand stance of condemnation – for those of you in this place, you may find that way down deep, if you take an honest look in the mirror, you may see that you were in some part responsible for the drama that ensued. When it is yourself you need to forgive, one large, looming creature usually stands in the way: guilt.

Letting Go of the Past

As we go through life, no one escapes without at least one incident from the past that plagues them. For example, I will share with you the story of one of my clients. Now in her fifties, she was having a terrible time with trust; she felt useless and incapable. In sessions we worked together and unraveled the fabric in order to get to the raw feeling of initial patterning, and I had to ask her about her first memory of fear (this being the catalyst for what initiated the unhealthy pattern).

What follows is how she described what had stayed with her for 45 years.

She came from a loving home. At the age of five, during her first year of kindergarten, she had a teacher who used to chastise her when she replied with a question and/or gave a wrong answer. This teacher would yell at her every time, saying she had all the wrong answers, then punish her by calling her stupid. Then she would be locked in a closet for what felt like forever. At intervals the teacher would open the closet door and tell the little girl that she was throwing spiders in the closet with her, and the classroom would laugh.

After she finished telling me her traumatic story, I told her that her problem surrounded the word "stupid." Because it was ingrained into her brain's belief system, she took that same energy with her everywhere. It was with her when her first husband would embarrass her and call her stupid, and in all the jobs she worked, where she would end up getting in fights and would inevitably get fired. All of this difficulty she had moving her life forward stemmed from the drag of this past trauma.

With this unveiling of negative initial patterning in childhood, this grown woman had a profound breakthrough to understanding. She works daily with positive affirmations to retrain her brain and now is living vibrantly in The YES Frequency.

So the thing to understand is that there is a pattern that has been set, and until you delete it, your subconscious is still going to run your show. And until you start to look at that as a shift that you want to make, it is not going to change. Please look within yourself and say, "I don't want to relive that nightmare anymore," and start to love yourself by acknowledging all the great things inside you. We all carry gifts in this lifetime. We all have special talents. We all have the ability to do anything. But often we forget, or we struggle with a continual little voice inside us that says, "You can't."

Have you ever had that voice that says "You're too old" or "They don't want you"? It seems to have endless negative things to tell you about yourself. You don't know enough. You're not smart enough. You're not handsome or pretty enough. You're a loser. This little voice is in your head somewhere, and what you have to do is change it with love.

If you are looking at yourself as if there is something wrong with you, get that idea out of your head, because every opportunity is a new beginning for you. That means with a new thought you can feel better and change your direction. But you must have a destination in mind in order to know where you want to point your compass.

Some people in life say, "Oh well, we will see what happens." Do you ever say that? Are you in that space in your life right now? Are you saying, "Oh, we'll see what happens"? This is not the same as a destination. You have to have a direct course and a clear picture of where you're going in order to set sail.

How many of you would get in a boat and set sail for a foreign country and say, "Well, we will see what happens"? I don't think you would get in a boat for such a journey, unless it was a proper boat with a captain, a crew, and computerized instruments to chart the course. Wouldn't you rather pick that boat than just a little sailboat with no destination? Or would you just get in the sailboat and say, "I'm going to take this trip with this guy and wing it, and we'll see where we are when we get there." You more than likely would not get there.

In life it is about choices. Taking the right action now to be the star of your own movie, you have to bring your consciousness into the forefront. And you have to have more fun in your life. Are you having enough fun in your life? Almost nobody is.

Find the balance to feeling good. The stability that comes with feeling good stems from eating right and exercising. Your body is your temple, and whether it's dancing, swimming, riding a bike, or yoga, it is up to you to do something to uplift your energy.

What we are really talking about is changing your energy and building into a forgiving frequency in order to effect transformation. The intention you hold inside yourself serves as a guide for what you really want to happen. So become clear as to what your intention is! Your intention may be about finding more love, or a new job, or creating a new life with a new husband or wife. But you must be clear; otherwise, you are just getting in that sailboat and floating.

Are you tired of floating? That can become boring very

quickly. Do you want to go full steam ahead? That feeling is the result of what we want to create. Now, your initial reaction may be, "How can I do that?" We have to move with the intention of knowing that it is already an end result – remember living "as if" – and say instead, "When I can do that!"

When you trust the universe, you trust yourself; if you haven't created your dream, there is a reason why. It just means you have been thinking the wrong thoughts, speaking the wrong words, talking to the wrong people, and maybe eating the wrong foods.

In order to attain your dream, you have to first have a dream. Some of you have forgotten your dream. If you have said, "Oh that's impossible," I am here to tell you that the impossible is possible. Have you ever experienced a miracle? They do exist. When you combine the miracles with the intention with the belief, you're going to start seeing results.

Sometimes guilt holds us back. Guilt is often accompanied by a false sense of responsibility for someone else. It's also accompanied by feelings of unworthiness. Like everything else, guilt may also serve a valuable purpose. It lets us know when we've done something that doesn't resonate with our soul. Many people thrive on slinging verbal hints and using guilt in between certain meanings as a way of manipulating a person or situation. This is another unnerving exploitation. Addressing that issue will need another chapter.

When it comes right down to it: Forgiveness is an act of LOVE.

You probably know this expression: "If you don't love and honor yourself, you can't love and honor anyone else." Forgiveness is one of the ultimate acts of self-love. Many people hold back forgiveness as a way to "punish" the person who wronged them. But in reality, the person you punish when you hold onto anger and resentment is yourself. How many times do you go back in time and rewind situations or dialogue, and replay it for yourself, when in truth it was so long ago that the script keeps changing and the shark keeps getting bigger?

Even if you can't yet fully inhabit this concept, for a few weeks try to act as if it is true – take on that role of being a forgiving character. This will actually lighten your heart. Say YES to this idea. You can always go back to being negative, but I guarantee that as you live in this frequency of forgiving, you will love life more, and it will change for the better all around you.

We may think we can gauge when the person who wronged us deserves our forgiveness, but consider all the energy that takes. Is it really worth it? Many of you have wasted years in this

> *"To forgive is to abandon your right to pay back the predator in his own coin, but it is the loss that liberates."*
> –Archbishop Desmond Tutu

cycle of anger. I know it's not working for you. Break the negative pattern your brain has been trained in and move to The YES Frequency of forgiving. Forgiveness sets you free.

Being forgiven by someone else is not what releases us from the pain of our wrongdoings; it's self-forgiveness that does that. You need to be able to look in the mirror and be honest with yourself – to admit what you've done, accept the consequences, feel the emotions that emerge, and then say to yourself, "I love myself. I forgive myself."

Punishing yourself or anyone else drains your energy and poisons your frequency – the frequency that is necessary for successful and healthy living for everyday life, and joy *forever*. When you refuse to forgive, your energy stays bound to the person you hurt or whom you feel hurt you. And until you cut the cords and release the burden of guilt, you will be stuck in the past, unable to move into the present, unable to live or love in the present. No good can ever come from that.

Recognize your humanity. Embrace your mistakes for the learning experiences they are. Each situation you find yourself in is an incredible gift, filled with opportunities for wisdom

> "Your living is determined not so much by what life brings you as by the attitude you bring to life."
> –John Miller

and learning. Embrace that gift and give yourself permission to forgive; if it is too difficult to do with love, try it with calm serenity, and the love will follow.

It is through humility and being real that you will come to remember that you deserve the gift of forgiveness – forgiving others and again, above all, forgiving yourself.

Breaking the Fear Factor

Here are some typical responses from my clients when I ask them what their biggest fear in life is:

- I am afraid of what is going to happen to me in the future.

- I am afraid of making changes in my life.

- I am afraid that I won't find a new job.

- I am afraid I will never meet my life partner.

- I am afraid I will not have enough money.

- I am afraid I won't have enough time.

- I am afraid I don't have enough energy.

DON'T LET FEAR GET IN YOUR WAY! Step right through it and keep moving forward. Some of you ask what you can do to change your life, to overcome fear, and to really start living an extraordinary life? Many of you have gone through enormous stress, emotional sabotage, and many other levels of disappointments, hardships, and nearly being scared to death. This is where the fear comes from.

In the twelve-step program for Alcoholics Anonymous, it is said that FEAR is simply an acronym that stands for "False Evidence Appearing Real!"

Indeed, if you really take the time to analyze your fears, you will usually begin to see that they are actually benign – you had simply blown them out of all proportion to reality. Let's jumpstart some changes, making "results" the goal that will override all fears.

Here's my first tip for you: Look for things to create. Sometimes our creative ideas and projects don't come to fruition, and that stems from our fear of what happened last time, what didn't happen, or what never happens. Guess what? You are not the only one! Fear can be like a boa constrictor that squeezes the virtual life out of you.

So if you are having a hard time getting out of your "old brain" way of thinking, return to your mission statement and say it out loud. Continue to be steadfast in believing in your mission statement and the values behind it. This will dissipate your fears and retrain your thinking to a positive focus. Replacing the negative pattern with a positive one will eradicate that inner voice of fear.

Take an honest look at what you think has been stopping you from truly creating, living, loving, and being inside The YES Frequency of life. Are you afraid of what people think? Is worry running your show? Are you afraid of what may or may not happen if … ? Are you afraid of the negative people whose fearful voices echo in your mind? The list of fear-mongering can go on forever. Stop wasting your brainpower on invisible negatives.

Letting go of the past by being willing to forgive can be a revelation. When you feel yourself transition from past influences to your present course, as dictated by your mission statement, you enter this flow and become saturated in The YES Frequency. When you do this, fear will be stamped out, and you will be free to live, enjoy, radiate, and smolder with satisfaction.

Once you feel this weightless feeling you will never want to carry the baggage of fear again. This glow will illuminate the way. So many open doors and new people will be attracted to your vibrant energy. When you stay constant, this creates your personal, indelible frequency of YES. In addition to the why of it all, there are a multitude of layers that we are unraveling to get to the core of the frequency in you.

Now, some of you may say, "I have already forgiven my ex" or "my ex-boss." "I'm not afraid of much of anything." "I forgive everyone for all their infractions against me." If you have completed these understandings with absolute resolution, excellent! Well done! I applaud you!

But if you have an undercurrent of angst and are not sure why, I have just one question for you: Is there one person you have skipped? Is it possible the reason you have not been able to soar ahead in life is because of that one person you completely neglected to understand? Is it possible that the one person you may have forgotten to forgive is YOU? Have you had a thread of fear inside you that you yourself may have had some part in the twists of life, in getting yourself where you are today? If so, let us be done with foolish fear and get rid of self-sabotage altogether.

The Power of Affirmation

Affirmations are usually things that we say or read in a repetitive way to give us a gentle reminder of where we want to be. The following affirmation, "The Golden Sun Ritual to Release All Fears," will help you visualize releasing fear by opening up to the healing power of the sun. You will be releasing any fears that have stood in your way. As you take a long, deep breath, and as you read on, let the words paint an image in your mind that will help you let go of fear.

If you need to, read the following into the answering machine on your cell phone or computer and play it back so you can hear your own voice telling you these things. Go to a place where you feel calm, whether inside or outside of your mind. Whatever form this takes for you, get comfortable and listen:

The Golden Sun Ritual to Release All Fears

- Visualize a warm golden light flowing into the top of your head, into both of your open hands, and into the soles of your feet. Breathe that golden energy into your whole body. It is filling every part of you. Notice it now, surrounding you with a beautiful golden cocoon…

- As you take another deep breath, feel how safe and loved you are. Breathe in the stillness and the silence.

- You've been holding onto a belief that has stood in the way until now. There is a fear that is ready to be released. That fear is asking right now, in this moment, for you to recognize it … Ask yourself the right questions.

- Taking a deep breath that is filled with confidence and love, ask the fear to come stand in front of you. Ask it to show you what it looks like.

- Notice the fear outside you. It is standing in front of you with a physical appearance and a name all its own.

- It is time to tell that fear that you have learned what you needed to learn, that you no longer need to hold onto the fear. As you tell the fear that it is no longer a part of you, affirm that today you are ready to let all of these fears go away. Watch the fear dissipate.

- Now the fear is only a tiny spot in front of you. Infuse the little speck with love and white light, releasing the fear completely.

- As you take a deep breath and begin to move out of this visual salutation, affirm once again: "I am free from all fear."

Just as forgiving releases all the drama and the trauma and pushes it out of our bodies, the same goes for fear. You just need to override the "scary movie" aspect of your thinking. Change the channel of your thoughts to the positive, the joyful; humor is always a buoyant way to let all negativity pop like a balloon. Fear will no longer slow you to a standstill, or lead you down the road to panic. We all know that those unnecessary feelings of doom and gloom don't enhance the outcome. Positive thinking truly does magnetize positive changes. In order for transformation to occur, leave the word "fear" where it belongs: in the dictionary.

We are born in a state of pure being, ready and open to experience all that life has to offer – beautiful beings birthed from spirit, ready to express this loving strength of mind through our shared individual experiences and there in our lives. I urge you not to let the fear that you carry with you stand in the way of your shining being.

Self-Sabotage

Fear can also act as a "front" for self-sabotage. The negative patterns have made their impressions inside you from habit, just like the way your feet create a footprint inside your shoes. Have you ever studied an old pair of flip-flops? You can see a perfect image of your foot along the bottom of the shoe. The negative patterns do this exact same thing in your mind, except we can't see the damage fear and self-sabotage create in the brain. The only way to recognize that it is not working for you is through the sheer example of your present moment: where your life is today.

To differing degrees, simply by being on the planet, we have been exposed to or involved in some sort of drama in our lives. At any point along our journey, we may have experienced various levels of emotional injury – everything from hurt feelings and fear to outrageous shock and physical trauma. These events register in both our psyche and our body. Unless we effectively release these injuries and the subsequent messages we give ourselves, drawing from this past experience, there remains a residual effect, which colors every day of our lives and all our future experiences, expectations, and relationships with others. Often, we do not even realize that we continue to carry these past experiences around inside us.

In many cases, this type of nonforgiving state can embed itself into your very core subconscious, the heart of your way of life. This is like a stain that discolors you and radiates to those around you. A stain like this will pull an individual completely away from the frequency that is desired.

Naturally, we all feel sorry for those who are in constant misery or are endlessly rehashing their complaints. This is not who you want to be or be perceived as, or be surrounded by. We create messages – inner dialogue – formed from our perceptions of these experiences. We repeat these messages over and over to ourselves until we believe them to be "truth." We come to believe that this is how the world is: full of hurtful or fearful situations and people with whom we are not able to establish trusting, open relationships. Or perhaps we internalize and personalize these messages differently, forming an opinion of ourselves that is less than stellar. Living in the past creates blocks and obstacles in the present.

Imagine how much better life could be if we simply recognized the joy and the bliss and the light that is our birthright, without carrying any additional overlay of past hurt, fear, sadness, or injury? This is not to suggest that we should live in a state of denial or unwillingness to see what we call "reality." Unpleasant and challenging things do happen in life. We all know this. What I am talking about is how we choose to view what we label "reality" and how we choose to experience and categorize the people, places, and circumstances of our lives. Stop blocking your own path in life. It's easy to spot this in someone else, but make sure to check for this in yourself, too. This needs to be about releasing the past and moving into the present.

We are powerful spiritual beings, with an innate ability to have deep input into the creation of our own lives. Living in a state of love and joy every day, even in the face of formidable tasks and seemingly overwhelming challenges, is the formula you want to adhere to.

Our inner spiritual awareness and the manner in which we view our experiences color our perception of reality on a daily basis. Are we living from that deep consciousness, that inner spiritual place of love and peace? Are we the protagonists of our own lives? Or just spectators watching through the layers of history, holding onto the past as if it were still happening?

If you find yourself in any of the following situations, consider that the past may still be operating in your perception of your daily life.

Testing Your PAST Barometer

- Is there a constant inner dialogue in which criticizing is rampant?

- Is ego stepping forward in an overt manner toward others?

- Is blame a larger part of the dialogue you utilize?

- In your conversations about your life, do you speak about the fault of others as a reason you may or may not be where you wanted to be?

- In certain circumstances, are you predestined to react harshly and negatively or to be judgmental as a first response?

- Is feeling fear or anxiety (when clearly not in a life-threatening situation) a regular part of your life, something you have made a habit of?

- Do you have expectations of others in which you do not clearly communicate issues that feel like disappointment?

- Are you still talking about the past with anger, disappointment, and blame?

- Do you embody the feeling from the past when you retell a past negative story?

Some strategies to releasing the past include ways to retrain your brain, leaving negative patterns behind. Consider the following questions:

- Are you consciously seeking and expressing spirit in all you do?

- Are sound, calm, and steady reactions ready tools in your ability to communicate?

- How responsibly do you react to taxing experiences, activities, and outcomes in your life?

- Are you energetic and enthusiastic about manifesting your desires?

- Are your actions, thoughts, and deeds filled with as much positive energy as possible?

- Do you have clarity when you express your desires, wants, or wishes?

- In the workplace, do you articulate and delegate in the same way you would like to be spoken to?

- When faced with adversity, do you usually take responsibility in a dignified fashion?

Even when encountering difficulties, isn't it astonishing to see how some people just become calm, focused, and present; there's something almost beautiful in how they confront adversity. Examine the above questions in your mind and strive to become what you admire in others.

3

The Self-Love Frequency

Love is a powerful force. It is an attracting energy. When you express love, it sets up a vibration that acts as a magnet to let the universe love you. We are powerless over people, places, and things. If we acknowledge that we have no control over others, we free up all that time and energy we've been spending on trying to change them, and we can now take back that lost energy and focus on ourselves.

It is time for you to give yourself permission to have power over your own life. Start nourishing and feeding yourself properly in *all* ways; start loving and respecting your body, mind, spirit, and soul as you submerge yourself in the frequency of love and all that it embodies.

As you move forward, use your mission statement as a touchstone, continuing with that goal in mind. In the greater design of your life, as you think of your lifetime achievements, refer to them as a great prequel to your story in this healthy mode of change. We will now build on moving forward with self-love and its frequency.

Isn't it wonderful when you know or see people who are "madly in love"? It is so beautiful. The blossoming stages of love are like a magic spell. In my experience, the healthier the people are inside themselves, the longer the spell lasts. The spell becomes diminished only when negative thinking infiltrates the mind. The patterns of your past, along with insecurity, ego, jealousy, and lack of trust, corrupt the magic spell like a virus disrupts a computer, and that's when things start to go south. We want to think that this must be Mr. Right or Miss Soulmate, but when the relationship falls into distant thunder, the feeling of happiness goes away.

We all want that feeling of loving and being loved, and I wouldn't trust anyone who didn't. The feelings of love move us forward. When love retreats, we often attach to the feeling so strongly that it erodes our self-assurance. We feel like we're lost. We don't want to open ourselves up to seeking new love, because even the thought of experiencing that pain again makes us feel empty. It is only when you place love and respect for yourself *first* that the doors will remain open to finding healthy love.

All relationships manifest for a reason. And yes, you may have to look for that reason, but if you find and hold that truth close to your heart and don't take it personally, that is a formidable head start to embodying real love.

We are ALL forms of varied love. Love comes in all shapes and forms, from a friend, to a family member, to all the traditional understandings of what love is. Love can be used the wrong way, though, and love like this will distort your frequency. When love is a game, or if it is used like a weapon, run for your life.

Should you yourself be the culprit approaching love this way, the inner truth about this manipulation will reveal itself to you in more and more destructive ways. For those of you who are in a love relationship that involves an abuse of power, or if you are in a cycle of victim-styled relationships, you must seek professional guidance through therapy to escape from these negative elements. Most abusive, narcissistic, psychopathic relationships never change. The only way to escape is to leave immediately and save yourself.

When you live in a healthy environment and trust in the divine order, the universe is attracted to that energy, and when sustained it lifts you into a love frequency that makes your vibrations a kind of fountain of youth. Love continually emanates from your true heart. It is the essence of life. Without love there really is no beginning or end. We enter this world with an unconditional understanding of love; conditioned love is something we have to learn – it is not innate. One never runs out of love, nor can you lose it. It may be dormant, but the vibration of love is always within reach. As you stay connected to this vibration, and are aware of making changes that bring on spiritual growth, you can now expand your consciousness and move forward to create your true potential, releasing anything and everything that does not harmonize with your being. In this way, you do not limit yourself to any conscious or unconscious restrictive beliefs.

Old habits are hard to break. We establish patterns, for better or worse, then we either set up more beneficial ways of living or we fall into a rut of redundant behavior. The bad news is, what we do regularly and repeatedly becomes a habit and can also take on a life or character of its own through this repetition. The good news is, the positive things that we repeat regularly will become a beneficial reality. Unfortunately, we spend most of our time putting ourselves in a constant state of unnecessary turmoil.

The signs are pretty clear – look within. As we start overreacting to stress, we begin blaming traffic, the kids, our boss, even the weather for the poor choices we make. The great news is, we possess the power to pull ourselves out of that state and change those negative patterns of behavior. At any time, we can make the decision to make a change.

In speaking and relating only to your positive thoughts, please appreciate yourself, your body, and your entire being. Yes, you are limitless and infinite. All of life can be seen as love. We are the source and supplier of an abundance of love. Love is the essence of what we are in the world. Your commitment to compassion and kindness is an avenue that will give you answers. Trust in your own authentic essence.

Your ability to create changes that you can believe in is yours as soon as you desire it. Surrounding yourself with positive, loving, evolved people will place you on the fast track to living inside the Frequency of YES and all it has to offer – living free and clear, in our authentic voice, in this present moment!

"Authentic voice" means honoring your own conscious awareness of how you feel, what you believe, what your desires are, and what expectations you have for yourself and others. This authenticity can only live in the present. Residing peacefully moment by moment will allow you full access to The YES Frequency. In truth, the present moment is the only reality we have. The past is gone; the future is merely anticipated and not guaranteed. The present is what we have in life, where we live in time. Our spiritual freedom and our natural state of awareness are expressed through living and speaking the truth. The truth resides within each of us, even when it doesn't always resound.

One of my clients had a terrific presentation of what she considered her way of thinking. Intellectually, she was brilliant and knew exactly how she felt, what was right, and so on. But emotionally, on the inside, she was shivering with indecision. Again, this goes back to brain training, and after a few sessions she was on track. She was able to go forward without doubt, and her continual self-examination changed into secure and positive YES Frequencies.

So allow your heart and soul to step forward, and with them the layers of experience that life has given you. Allow yourself to feel gratitude and peace – these are the feelings that best embody the Frequency of YES. They are the antidotes to negative messages and allow you to let go of negativity, which serves no useful purpose.

You must get to know your emotions intimately, and take

responsibility for them, if you want to avoid miscommunications or mistaken beliefs. Your goal is to keep moving toward ending the negative repetitions in your life, and replacing them with positive affirmations. By regularly repeating and reinforcing positive thoughts, words, and messages, you eventually change your inner dialogue for the better.

As you pull up the anchor and start the process of releasing and letting go, removing blocks and obstacles within yourself, you will feel a floating way of life envelope you. Setting sail is the goal. The first step is to identify belief systems and messages derived from your traumatic past experiences and say goodbye to them once and for all.

Hang onto those people who support you in a positive, uplifting, and loving manner. If the people in your life are not supporting you in this way, challenge their negative beliefs and dialogue, then let go of people who no longer relate to you in a positive way.

Sometimes, you can stop people being negative by constantly and calmly reinforcing the positive. Being negative all the time is exhausting, and you have a role to play in shifting your perceptions and beliefs to those that support and enhance not only your life but the lives of all those you touch.

Practice reinforcing these messages in every activity you do, in every conversation you have with others, and in your inner monologue. Your inner monologue is what lays down the track for the thoughts that are projected into the universe, its frequency. You are your own frequency, so take note of all that you say, and think optimistically before you speak.

Take a few minutes every day to align with Spirit, to give thanks, to acknowledge your new and improved beliefs, and find ways to see these beliefs at work in your life. Live in your joy and bliss. Share this positive and loving energy with each fellow being you encounter, as we all continue to grow and learn and expand together.

The Subconsious versus the Conscious Mind

If you are still holding back and not yet ready to leap into the exuberance of The YES Frequency, let me help you to take a deeper look at yet another layer of the subconscious mind.

The subconscious mind doesn't negate anything – it absorbs everything that is being said, like a child.

Let me give an example.

Let's pretend I said I was going to lock you up in my living room for a week, and during that whole time I was going to play you bad music and show you negative images, so that negative words were disrupting your thoughts and sleep. If you experienced that for days on end, with no break, do you know what would happen? When you were finally released you would feel like a walking disaster, a tornado inside.

But if I did the same thing, locking you up in my house for the same amount of time and I kept saying YES to you – if I kept giving you positive affirmations and sharing good energy, meditation, beautiful music, stunning images, positive words, comfortable surroundings, healthy food, and cozy sleeping quarters – guess what would happen? You would go outside and, because your subconscious had been retrained, miracles would happen. This is because you would be on the miracle frequency, the miracle tram. It would be called the M line. Everywhere you would go, you would take this feeling with you.

It is not too late to make a change and get back on track – or in some cases, start a new program for yourself and set up more beneficial ways of living. No more ruts of destructive people or behavior. What you do is totally up to you. No more blaming the ex, the kids, traffic, your boss, laundry, the weather, or your mother-in-law for the poor choices you've made. Gone are the days of placing ourselves in a "victim" mentality. Gone are the hours of spiritual malnourishment. You possess the power to live inside a healthy brain and self.

Today is a new page, a new day, a fresh start. Through your

mission statement, your purpose has been established.

How easy was that? This is not brain surgery. In this moment you have everything necessary to reconstruct your mindset, and your reality will follow. The time is NOW – this very moment. There is nothing stopping you or holding you back but the old patterns of your thinking.

Some people say it takes a twenty-one-day cycle to successfully break a habit. Others say it takes a lifetime and a village of vigilance to keep you from falling back into long-established, unhealthy patterns of behavior and response. The twelve-step program used by Alcoholics Anonymous (AA) may have it said rather well: "One day at a time." This approach is the most realistic, because it acknowledges the constant challenge to stay in the moment.

You know you deserve this! Experience the feeling of greatness right inside you this very second. As you read this, with every breath you are uncovering new gifts and more layers in your endless capacity for embodying The YES Frequency.

During your day, pay attention to any negative influences or questions or unsupportive voices from the past that come forward. Notice how much is percolating in your thoughts on a daily basis.

What would happen if you could release every fear, every doubt, and every pressure in your life and replace it with the feeling of love? You would be free to live the life you have always longed for. This is not a dream. This can be a reality. You can be free this very second – free to release all blocks and barriers, letting go of anything you perceive as preventing you from living in the now. If you knew your time on this earth was limited, what would you change today? You can create the life you want in this very moment by stepping into the frequency of love.

I will share with you an example of dedication. This kind of accomplishment is metaphorically the same in long-distance competitive swimming. It's called "breaking the pain barrier."

In aggressive distance swimming, you have 66 laps to complete (1,650 yards/U.S. and 800 meters in a 50-meter pool that meets "Olympic standards"). After 33 laps, you are at a breaking point – either hitting a wall and struggling or breaking through that wall. If you can break the pain barrier, you will enter this euphoric energy; you will be focused inside "the zone," which connects you to a powerful vigor. The feeling is comparable to a new start that catapults you forward, and that is where you will be when you get inside The YES Frequency.

Life Key Code

Most of us have experienced the ability to accomplish more than we thought we could, but this is only part of the possibilities that await us. The other part of the "doing" calls on us to trust that we have help from the entire universe.

Confidence

Disempowering habits affect your confidence and are direct roadblocks to the furtherance of your goals. Everyone has confidence; the difference is to what degree. Remember, you are changing old, disempowering habits for new, empowering ones. At first this may make you feel off balance and insecure. Your instinctive reactions are going to go through your new internal editing positive mechanism as well. Each day you do the work you are gaining confidence and strength.

Before we continue, I want you to have a clear vision for your life. Take a moment and spend some quiet time on your own to think about what is happening in your life right now. What parts are working, and what parts are not working? What parts of yourself and your life do you like, and what parts would you like to change? Confidence is what I want you to carry forward.

Make a list of the problems that seem to be recurring issues:

_____

_____

_____

_____

What things do you feel might be blocking your success?

_____

_____

_____

_____

In order to love your life, your job, your friends, and your family, you must love, honor, and respect YOURSELF first. A big part of this is forgiving yourself for any past decisions that you may believe have hindered the present state of your life.

With confidence in your mission statement and your values, try the following exercise.

Write out the positive solutions to each issue you face:

_____

_____

_____

_____

What do you believe about yourself? If you were asked, would you say you think you are a worthwhile person, deserving of all the good that life has to offer? Chances are, you would answer in the affirmative, as most of us would. This is the message you would give the world.

Remain confident in the message you would tell yourself –

the one that would reveal what you truly believe about yourself! Do you have a propensity to insult yourself when things go wrong? Imagine that you dropped the ball, forgot a due date, or lost something of a friend's. What would you say to yourself? Would you tell yourself that you're human, that you were tired, that it happens to everyone, it's no big deal, that you should let it go? Or would you berate yourself, call yourself an idiot, a dolt, pathetically brain dead? Would you use the word "stupid" in your assessment of yourself, and even resort to vulgarities when referring to yourself?

So many of us automatically send ourselves these kinds of messages when we're not performing well in our everyday lives. And most of the time, we're not even aware what we're programming into our subconscious mind, which, as I mentioned, acts like a sponge, soaking up everything.

When we flub a line during a work presentation, don't get the job we applied for, or are stood up for a date, what do we tell ourselves about ourselves at those times? That we're fabulous, that we did the best we could, that we'll do better next time, that the right job or the right partner is on the way? Chances are, the message we send ourselves is the same as the one we transmit when we miss the train or, worse, the plane. It may be comical, but rarely pretty.

While it's important to look at our mistakes and find ways to make improvements, it is not in our spiritual, emotional, physical, or psychological best interest to use these mistakes as an excuse to put ourselves down.

We would never speak to a loved one or even a stranger the way we talk to ourselves when we err. Would you call a dear child an idiot for forgetting to buy milk at the store? Never! This kind of parenting is disgraceful. Would you walk up to someone on the street and say they were mentally challenged because they had different-colored socks on? Would you tell a good friend that they're no good and will never get ahead if they didn't get that promotion at work? Certainly not! But this is how way too many of us talk to ourselves way too much of the time. It might seem petty, but this kind of negative chatter is a form of verbal abuse.

This is a great example of when you can go back to the earlier chapter and insert the forgiveness frequency, by apologizing to yourself and others. Say you're sorry to the person or people that you disrespected, then forgive yourself for the transgression. We may think it's harmless to castigate ourselves in this way when we don't do things perfectly, but each time we engage in such behavior, we are reinforcing unconstructive beliefs all around.

Holding ourselves to impossible standards and inflicting punishment for failing to live up to unrealistic expectations is not useful and doesn't help us move forward as individuals. When people expect things from themselves that are outside their capabilities, they set themselves up for failure. Most of the time, when you have expectations of an event or a person, it places you in a judgment seat. This is dangerous territory, keeping you far away from The YES Frequency.

If you have children, you must set rules and discipline them when they break them in order to teach boundaries. That said, if this is done in an arbitrary way, you can damage a child's inner confidence.

At the other extreme are parents who buy their children's affection because they themselves are so insecure, so desperate for love and affection, that they have *no* boundaries, allowing their children to run wild. This is a serious detriment to their children's future. When a child does not feel a balance of boundaries, they feel out of control, and inside they desire a parent's involvement and calm, closely controlled order. It is a teenager's natural path to buck the system; it is a parent's duty to rein them in with love and consistency.

You need to wield love the same way when you are talking to yourself. Note the messages you give yourself. And if you slip and castigate yourself, go as far as writing it down, like a citation! This will help keep you from repeating these infractions, because it will help you pay attention to your inner vernacular. After a few days, sit down and read what you have written. Make a note of the derogatory terms you have heaped on your very precious being.

Burning Ceremony

Close your eyes and ask that you be willing to surrender this need to be so unkind to yourself. Write down all castigations on pieces of paper. Then find a safe place to light a fire, and burn the pieces of paper and the dreadful words written on them.

Afterward, should you make any kind of error, say the following to yourself: "No comment." Get this phrase in before your negative belief system can feed you any offensive words of self-description, then continue on your way. With time, you will notice that the list of horrible terms you use for yourself will become shorter. Repeating "No comment" will keep you in a neutral space, accepting your blunder but not using it to condemn yourself.

Changing our belief system is a daunting task. It requires commitment to action. At times, we cannot think our way into right actions; we have to take action into right thinking. Ask yourself each time you are filled with self-loathing, "What is the right action for me to take? What might I do to change this unhelpful thinking?"

The key is to do things you can truly applaud yourself for. Volunteer for a local charity. Visit a sick friend and make the conversation all about them. Donate blood. Volunteer at a retirement home. Help the needy. Go through your closet and give all those old clothes to a charitable home for those in need. In order to find and recognize the good in ourselves, we often have to lose ourselves in "right actions." The feeling we get from making philanthropic contributions is totally uplifting.

Our self-perception changes each time we make a decision to make a positive contribution to our lives, and moreover, to the lives of others. Start feeding your spirit and YES Frequency *today*.

Are you in tune with this frequency? If you have an undercurrent of reservation, think about this. Too often we wait for something to stop us sharply in our tracks, jolting us to wake up. Sadly, this often comes in the form of a tragedy, loss, or devastation.

In many instances this is because it takes radical situations to get our attention. You have heard the expression "hitting rock bottom." You do not have to wait for that to happen. You can make today the first day of your new life, simply by deciding that it will be so. Every moment matters – each and every moment is a special moment, never to be experienced again.

Life Key Code

We are all beings of consciousness; everything that we are and do begins with our thoughts

The Power of Questions

We have examined many of the issues surrounding The YES Frequency, and now you are ready to continue to move forward. Here's something to think about first. If it's so easy to get the results we want, why do we wait so long? Avoidance and sheer procrastination! We love to keep ourselves busy – that way, we don't have to ask why our situation isn't working.

Stop filling your time with nonsense, and start setting priorities. Be more efficient. What are the things you want to accomplish? Why are you not spending your time accomplishing them? Interesting question, isn't it? Here is where the excuses usually start. Mind over matter – audit your thinking and stop saving the world before you save yourself. Think about the safety video on an airplane. You must secure your own oxygen mask first, so that you can be effective for those around you. Parents, this is for you especially! I know you think, "Oh no, I must help little Lily first." What you are not thinking about is, if you pass out, little Lily has no one to help her!

Take back your power, and stop giving yourself away. Raid the enemy of your mind, which is negativity. Deactivate the bomb that clouds your vision to achieve your own goals. What are some of the most common excuses for everything we are not doing?

"I am too busy."

Are you really? Too busy to make time for yourself, and moreover, for your goals? You must make time to put your mission statement into action.

"I am too tired."

Self-discovery is hard work. Happier people force themselves to face their issues and ask the right questions. We have no problem answering questions that other people ask us. Why are you happier knowing more about other people than about yourself?

Entertainment magazines that announce every celebrity's downfall contribute enormously to negative brain training. It is catastrophic for any of us to contribute to these money-grabbing leeches. Does it really make anyone feel better about his or her own life to know that someone else is suffering?

If you do enjoy those "paparazzi bottom-feeders," that says something about you needing to radically change the synapses of your thinking. Being intrigued by that kind of useless entertainment prevents you from entering the fluid YES Frequency in your own life. What you read, what you buy into, and what you spend your time doing is all a "vibrational" interchange. Pay close attention to what you are a part of. While you are working to change your vernacular, ask yourself what you are really taking away from your entertainment sources and start to look within.

"I'll get to it later."

"When I can find the time." "When I lose the weight." "When the kids graduate from school." "When I find the right person." "When I make more money." The variations of the excuses on this list are endless. Procrastination is an excuse that will keep you off track in perpetuity.

"I am afraid of what change may bring."

You should be more afraid of waking up ten years from now feeling the same way you feel right now. You are never too young or too old to be creative and imaginative. Be bold and brave. Just do it! What is the worst that can happen if you make this change? You can always return to your old patterns of behavior and thinking – but I don't think you will want to.

"I don't believe I can get more, so why ask?"

If you don't ask, you will never know. By not asking, you have already given up. Start learning the difference between disempowering questions and empowering questions. Here are a few examples:

DISEMPOWERING NEGATIVE QUESTIONS

1. Why me?

2. Why can't I be rich?

3. What is wrong with me?

4. When will my life change?

EMPOWERING POSITIVE QUESTIONS

1. Am I happy with the way my life is going?

2. Am I doing work that is satisfying and fulfilling?

3. Am I doing everything I can do to improve my situation?

4. Am I taking responsibility for my decisions?

See how much better you feel when you ask the right questions in the right way? I think 95 percent of the people in the world have no answers to these questions. They wander aimlessly through life, not knowing who they are. Have you fallen into this category?

The right questions will lead you on the path to discovering what you really want to happen in your life. Your statements and questions have an enormous power and impact, because they are either moving you toward a future that excites you, or toward a future that is full of a kind of "status quo." We need to learn how to reframe the questions you are asking yourself in order to help you jump into the correct frequency.

DISEMPOWERING NEGATIVE QUESTIONS

Why me?

When one is in a downward spiral of negativity, it is usually kick-started by the "Why Me" manner of thinking. And I promise you, this way of thinking is never going to benefit you in any way, shape, or form. You will only compound your problem by reinforcing this kind of verbiage in your everyday life. So if you are in any way stuck with this "poor me syndrome," I'm here to tell you *no one* is going to want to be in the vicinity of this kind of victim-mentality negativity! They are not going to want to spend time with you or invest in anything you have to offer. So stop!

Why can't I be...?

Are you reinventing the negative wheel by just changing one negative expression for another? Please spare yourself the "pity party" – it is a party *no one* will attend.

What is wrong with me?

Have you ever noticed that when negativity is combined with self-depreciation, questions like this never really seek constructive criticism. We all know the answers to our own self-deprecating questions, so STOP putting them out there. Think back to a time when you tried to help someone and what happened. People usually have about five hundred excuses as to the why of it all. Somewhere they have patterned themselves to such a negative degree that they actually don't want you to help them diagnose their problems and search out a way to better the situation. They just want to stay stuck in the tornado of misery.

Remember, you can only help those who want to help themselves, so take a look in the mirror if any of the above sounds familiar. You need to restructure your *entire* way of thinking into a new frequency!

EMPOWERING STATEMENTS

These are statements that empower you to reach your destination of choice. If you are living in a satisfied place in your life, this is wonderful.

Those who are happy and are expanding the horizons of their thinking will reap higher levels of contentment, opening more doors and being introduced to new people and situations. Reaching higher levels of enlightenment compels one to share more ways of enlightened thinking.

Read the empowering statement below and repeat it to yourself whenever you catch yourself using the language of disempowerment and negativity.

"I am doing everything I can do to improve my situation!"

Now it is a matter of sustaining the layers you have learned and making sure that you are in a positive state of mind, so much so that, in time, any negative influence that comes hurling at you will just fly past. Your frequency of YES will deflect any attempt to derail you.

Tone

As we continue to reframe the way in which we speak, our tone affects us and others. When you change the way in which you formulate words, you will also want to use a new tone. Just like music, this tone will create a new and open way in which your thoughts will affect you and those around you. Those who have known you for years will hear the absolute YES Frequency infiltrate the room. Listen as others will take to your calming tone.

Below are two more empowering approaches you can use to relate to others and your situation every day.

Ask advice from people who know!

Asking advice is a wonderful and empowering gesture that makes everyone happy. Why? Because advice is free, and asking for advice means you are willing to listen and heed the wisdom of someone whom you respect. No one asks advice from people they don't respect, do they? Of course not. Advice is something we all share with one another, and it is a beautiful exchange.

Relish investigating all choices.

When you are faced with a choice, dig deep and research all the choices that are available to you. Research is so much easier these days. Now, with technology, there is no excuse for not finding the direction you need to take. And even if you don't have a computer, you can go to the public library and seek help there. Most libraries have a multitude of volunteers and free computers you can use to access information that will take you where you want to go. Maybe best of all, the information you seek is likely available in all languages.

To help keep the doors open and get positive results, you will need to constantly reframe your questions. The following three steps are powerful tools to help strengthen your daily words and actions. These are essential in order to get to the core of what is reinforcing your belief system.

Step 1: Have a Positive Attitude

Everything will work out for the highest good. Be aware of your thoughts, and only speak the positive ones. Love yourself, your body, and your whole being.

Step 2: You Are Limitless and Infinite

The supply is truly limitless and is directly associated with love. All life can be seen as love! This is truly the essence of what we are in the world. The ways in which you are learning to love yourself and your life are expressed in the ideas and experiences you have.

Step 3: Personal Excellence and Commitment

Trust that you are the best. Choose to surround yourself with like-minded, evolved people. Make choices that move you into greatness! This commitment requires that you step from "I hope it happens" into "It will happen!"

Life Key Code

Love is the experience of oneness, a union of the mind and heart.

Surrender to Love

Remember that first "blush of a grade school crush"? The joy that radiated through you when you were inside that feeling? Think of the first memory where you surrendered to love – the "head in the clouds" feeling, the "blushing bride" syndrome, or that first "Cupid's arrow" feeling. Do you recall the kind of "rush to love" sensation that has you burning toast and forgetting to turn off the bathwater, because your state of mind is so heightened by love?

Today's technology has all of us looking at our phones all the time, so much so that people are walking into poles and tripping, falling down stairs, and not only crashing into one another but losing the art of conversation and social graces, and as a result they slowly become obsolete.

So many of us are neglecting and abusing our minds and bodies because we are too tired, overworked, stressed out, and overburdened with responsibilities. We are not in contact with love, nor its frequency, nor the intelligence of the universe. The less we care for our physical and conscious nature, the more we become alienated from our metaphysical nature. These God qualities are the integral part of you; they lie deep within you, whether you admit it or not.

These days, our world is filled with a constant barrage of data. The Internet, television, iPods, Blackberries, cell phones – all the technology that supports and aids us can also overwhelm us and sometimes put us in a constant state of anxiety. Where is the next e-mail? Who can I call now? What music can I listen to? What television show can distract me? We lack the ability to simply sit with ourselves, just be, and connect with the spiritual power that feeds us and fuels us. This spiritual power reminds us that we are part of something unknowable, something that is larger than ourselves and our hi-tech toys.

You are a content and powerful being. You are nothing less than an extraordinary force of nature. Clarity is power. Once you know what you desire, the path can be open to you, once you have passed through all the layers in order to access The YES Frequency.

The steps up to this point have led you to clarity – knowing what you desire – and moving into love. How easy it should be now, to manifest what you want to create.

Go straight to the end result. In order to become what you desire, you must be it – remember living "as if." You need to give yourself end results. Rather than showing up in a relationship or at a job with the wishy-washy energy of the middle, show up with the end result energy. The energy you show up with is what creates your life.

When you think the thoughts of a powerful being, knowing that's who you truly are and that you are love, you manifest things immediately. Trust yourself. Trust the universe. When you're not trusting, you're back in the middle. When you're worrying, you're back in the middle. A powerful tool for moving out of the middle into the end result is to constantly affirm "I AM LOVE."

Love is the highest vibration there is; it is the most powerful energy in the universe. So when you live in the energy of I AM LOVE, you show up with higher vibrations and you attract higher vibrations.

As you stay in that space, watch what happens. As you live in the energy of I AM LOVE, you will start to notice how everything around you shifts. Notice how empowered and confident you become. Keep affirming The YES Frequency inside love. The middle questions and fears and worries will disintegrate as the end result manifests itself.

Life is so extraordinary and magical when you operate from this high-vibrating energy that everything is possible. When you stay in the end result and believe in it, you make it happen. You create that reality. As you affirm to yourself I AM LOVE, you become love, and everything around you becomes a manifestation of that frequency. You are love. Believe it. Live it. Be it.

It begins with an intention. Say to yourself, "I love myself," then let the rest go. Do you feel the shift in energy when you say or think those three words? It's happening. Your energy is shifting each time you say or think, "I love myself." It's releasing baggage and washing away what was never yours to begin with; it's opening up spaces, making room for happiness and success.

As you say "I love myself," the color of your energy is shifting. It's becoming brighter, more vibrant. You begin to radiate the light you've seen in others – the light you've been attracted to. And you understand now why you were so mesmerized by people who had that certain something you yearned for. It's about self-love. You've had love all along. You only need to re-mind yourself. Say it again and again, "I love myself," and watch as your world shifts. The impossible becomes possible, what was complicated becomes simple, and confusion disinte-grates, replaced by profound clarity.

It's not difficult – it doesn't need to be. That's the beauty of it. Why shouldn't it be easy? All it takes is intending it. It's a choice. A decision. We make hundreds of decisions every day. This one, the decision to simply say "I love myself," will en-hance your life forever.

Some people have a glass-is-half-full personality; others have a glass-is-half-empty personality. The choice seems rather simple, doesn't it? It is simply about choosing one point of view over the other. That will set you apart.

The frequency of self-love approach teaches you to stay in the moment, not letting your mind focus on regrets about the past or fear of the future; you learn how to stay in the now, and in doing so, use the knowledge you gain. In order to achieve this, you need to start using the right language and build your subtext with love in order to create a greater result.

Let's start at the beginning. Every word you choose creates a cause and effect, for every thought will result in a mind frame in which your state of being continues to affect your behavior.

This behavior is contagious. If you are filled with joy and compassion and creative energy, this will cause those around you to be filled with a similar positive reaction. Doing this will provoke deep thought while inspiring concentrated reflection. As people receive and respond to your positive energy, the energy they reflect will affect you in turn. New doors will open, clarity will appear, and change will begin.

Life Key Code

A successful life depends on a foundation of self-trust, self-love, and self-belief.

Gratitude

Gratitude is about appreciating all the things in your life. In vibration with the positive, empowering thinking we've talked about, begin to notice what's right instead of what's wrong, and be grateful.

Shifting energy into being totally in gratitude and grace is rather like entering one of those brilliant classical music "flash mobs," where one person starts to play an instrument, then another, and suddenly you recognize the music to be a piece by Vivaldi as the street square fills with more and more musicians, making you feel you are in the mid-1700s.

When we each stand in our choice without judging the choices of others, it is then that we are empowered creators and inspire others to trust their own choices. Life is a work-in-progress, and in each moment we have the choice to be renewed, refreshed, and ready to move forward in the presence of each other.

The journey toward true soulful enlightenment, freedom, and success begins with looking at the self. Realizing who we are deep in ourselves helps us move to the bigger-picture view of life, seeing ourselves and recognizing our oneness with the universe. When we are in a feeling of gratitude the universe is open to sanctioning our frequency to gain momentum.

You must stand firm in gratitude and refuse to surrender to doubt or fear. This simple act opens your conscious connection to your soul's love and reassurance and allows you to let new things and conditions come into your life.

Take this feeling of gratitude with you as you journey through life and you will feel like you are traveling in first class. You will feel blessed just to be present in this moment as you view all that surrounds you. People will note the tone of your words and sense the calm and centered being behind them. The gratitude that you have encountered in your life comes through you now and opens new doors. Calm acceptance and a feeling of love are contagious.

Part Two
Reconfigure Your Behavior

4

The Purification Frequency

We have established that being attached to negative behavior is addictive to the brain. In such

> "An unmanaged mind will return to its old beliefs."

cases, we are predisposed to make choices based on patterns that seek out unnecessary drama. Could all of this be because you have set a pattern in your thinking that anticipates the worst? If your everyday life is conditioned by a psyche attuned to problematic behaviors, then like a drug addict you must stay away from that pattern. Our brains are addicted to following the thought configurations they are used to.

Attachment to Negative Behavior

Why aren't you feeling excited and enthusiastic about life? Ask yourself the following questions.

- Under what circumstances do I most notice my negative self-talk?

- Who and what triggers me to thinking in this negative pattern?

Note the times of day the negative chatter is the strongest. Is the chatter strongest when you are in conversation with certain people? Or is it when you lay your head on the pillow at night to go to sleep? Maybe it's on your way to work. Try and truly listen to the words creating your thoughts. These undercurrents of thought are the score that set the tone for how you interact in your life. This affects not just you but all those around you.

Think of this just like the soundtrack in a movie. If the music is uplifting and cheerful, it can make you want to dance; if it is slow and filled with dark and dramatic sharp tones, it can make you feel pensive or afraid. Create the sound score for your life by utilizing beautiful thoughts and sounds in your thinking. This creates not only the tone of your voice but the tone of your frequency.

After doing some undercover work on yourself for a day, I want you to sit down and make a note of the tone you used during the day. Were you harsh with your criticism of yourself? If so, close your eyes and say, "I surrender this need to be unkind to myself!"

Every day we use words that help create and define our lives. Negative words and sharp tones do nothing for us, except perpetuate negative results. You have more control over your own life than you ever thought possible.

I can hear you protesting right now, "What control? I had no control over the downsizing at my company and the loss of my job. I had no control over my mother blaming me for everything that is wrong with her life. I had no control over my house being invaded by bees." Obviously! These were events that occurred in your life. But what you *can* control are your emotional reactions to these events and the decisions you make after having those reactions.

It is perfectly normal to be upset when bad news arrives. Mourning any kind of loss is an important and vital part of the emotional process that allows you to move through difficult times. Everyone expresses their feelings in their own way. It's not healthy to suppress these feelings, just as it is not healthy to "act out" inappropriately.

It's important to have a support system in place, composed of trusted friends and counselors who can offer aid and understanding during tough times. When difficult times occur and it feels like things are out of control, take control. Get to the gym, eat a balanced diet, and confide in people you trust; scream in a pillow; but don't fall into the self-destructive trap of thinking you could have prevented something over which you had no control.

Most of us are unaware of the effect of tone in words and conversation, even though this moves people during the course of any given day. This tone is also in mind-chatter, and influences our end results. Think of this like cell phone ringtones. Which ringtone personifies your character? Have you noticed that some people have ringtones that are closely similar to that individual's character? Choose a speaking tone that emulates your new frequency, one that embodies a calm and joy-filled expression.

Words are the equivalent of tools with which we build our reality. To change our lives, we must change our tone within words. We speak and think thousands of words every single day, and the quality of these words and their tones are defining our lives. We can hear it in others, but we need to listen within.

Stay on course and combat any and all negative tones. You know how! Trust that you can implement the tools you have been given thus far.

This next exercise will help you become aware of the words that are defining your life. Even the words that you use in the questions you ask yourself and others must embody the correct subtext, so that you maintain your level in the purification frequency. When asking questions, state a positive outcome. Write as you expect it to happen, so your subconscious mind can allow this subtext into your conscious mind.

Example of a Negative Question: *Why are horrible things always happening to me?*

Example of a Positive Question: *Am I doing all the right things that will give me opportunities to change my life for the better?*

Once you frame the positive question, you will find the life-affirming answer is very clear. Start writing out the questions that plague you, but make sure you write them with an optimistic connotation.

_____

_____

_____

_____

Life Key Code

We do not create energy; we distribute it. And we know that we can transform energy from one type to another.

Eliminate the Anger

Anger is more often than not a symptom of profound disappointment. In many cases, it can also represent a feeling of inferiority or an inability to express frustration in an educated or controlled way. Sometimes it's just an instance of someone being emotionally arrested: during their development stages as a child, they were not taught or given the example of how to handle life's challenges. Their parental examples were a cluster of bad "acting out" examples. This makes children grow up, to a greater or lesser degree, socially inept. The individual acts out with anger and rage. We see it behind the wheel with the concept of "road rage." Those who feel powerless in their lives act out because in their car, they feel safe acting on their impulses. Or they lash out at people who are stuck behind the bank teller cages because the "worker" has been taught that the customer is to be handled respectfully.

This is also an abuse of power. What all this anger reveals is a profound lack of psychological education combined with a lack of self-worth, which is usually at the core of all of this. Being deficient in self-love usually happens because the individual was to some extent not given healthy love as a child, and therefore, without ever having a good example, they did not learn self-love. This treatment, or lack thereof, has these children growing up to be "anger-aholics," often because they feel comfortable with the reaction they were raised with. A person either grows up to be completely against that reaction and they fight that inclination in themselves, or they embrace it because it is what they find familiar.

There is always a lesson within the feeling of anger. Take a moment to analyze the levels of your anger. The healing frequency is waiting for you to answer. When you get angry, take a look within yourself and embrace the lesson. In more cases than not, anger toward friends and loved ones or fellow workers always snaps back to the idea of feeling "less than." Know that you are worthy and have the ability to release and heal your anger without lashing out at others.

This brings us back to square one: true forgiveness. If you have done the work of forgiving, then you will have instant access to the frequency to handle anger.

It is much more painful *not* to do the work, and to remain wrapped in anger and resentment. There is a strong and clear motivation for learning the lessons within your impulse to anger: you clear the way for miracles in your life. Holding onto anger and resentment costs only you, because it seals you off from love.

Forgiveness heals you and opens up space for love in your life. It allows your energy to move freely in uplifting directions. You have nothing to lose but the anger.

The words you choose have the power to move you forward or backward. The next step toward achieving success in this purification frequency is to be aware of your words during the most challenging moments in your life. Words are powerful tools. They are the fuel that moves you forward in life. The next time that you encounter any problematic issue, know that you hold the tools to eradicate any first response and release all feelings of irritation that are not constructive. I promise once you are in this frequency, you will never leave it again.

Life Key Code

All ideas and words are blueprints for something new in our lives. Fill your mind only with positive thoughts, and become the master of your own divine radiant expression.

It is hard to escape the harsh memories of having been chastised, bullied, or spoken down to. Undoing these negative influences will be a process. If you have a lapse and forget, you are not allowed to punish yourself for using negative words. When you find yourself thinking or saying a negative word, or using a negative tone, remember to say in its place (nicely), "No comment." This will derail your negative belief system. Follow this immediately with a positive word or thought.

Here are a few of the positive thoughts you may use to derail your negative self-beliefs:

- I am honest.

- I am loving.

- I am compassionate.

- I am inspiring.

- I am joyful.

See how these words evoke a different feeling? See how they create a powerful feeling inside you? Remember: you are human. You are not faultless; you will make mistakes. But when you do, stop calling yourself names. As we move forward, keep writing down the negative words you use to describe yourself, and shred or burn the list every few days. With time, the list will become shorter. Remember the Burning Ceremony in Chapter Three. Reread that section of the book whenever you need to.

When you say "No comment," give yourself permission to examine any mistakes you've made to determine if they are just singular events or if they are part of a pattern. If you decide that there is indeed a pattern to any set of errors, you are free to make the necessary changes.

For instance, if you are late to work and appointments because you are constantly misplacing your car keys, rather than calling yourself stupid, you can put a hook by your door and hang your keys there when you come home. Taking this positive action will not only help prevent you from being late but will bring more order to your daily routine. It will keep you positive by creating emotional homeostasis – a balanced state where you are no longer "less than" or "not good enough."

Remember: once you have spoken certain words aloud, you cannot take them back. It is important to choose empowering, loving, positive words. Every word has a cause and effect, and contributes to an end result.

Now I'm going to show you how, through reinforcing statements, you can activate The YES Frequency within seven days and change your life.

7 Days to Activate the Yes Frequency

There is a power in the universe, and you can use it. What you admire and acknowledge increases the flow of energy.

Practice speaking these principles each day to nourish your soul.

Day 1: Have a Solid, Positive Attitude

Know that everything works for the highest good. Be aware of your thoughts, and only speak higher positive ones. Love yourself, your body, and your whole being.

Day 2: You are Limitless and Infinite

Supply is directly associated with love. All life is love! Love is the essence of what we are. Loving yourself and loving life means being excited about all your ideas and experiences.

Day 3: Activate Desire and Clarity

Map out a plan (for example, a mission statement) of exactly what you see yourself being and doing. Learn to ask specifically for whatever it is you desire. Have a clear map of what it looks like.

Day 4: Align with Personal Excellence and Commitment

Trust that you are the BEST, and choose to surround yourself with only enlightened people. Make choices that move you into GREATNESS! Commitment requires that you step from "I hope it happens" to "YES, that's for me" and "It always works."

Day 5: Support Yourself and Give

Take action in creating an ongoing flow of money and abundance coming to you at all times. Give abundantly, without fear or thinking you might lose anything. Fear will stop you. Change the thought and belief. Take an action item that supports this new thought. Contribute a tithe.

Day 6: Trust

Learning to trust yourself and universal principles is difficult. But if you learn to live in this way, you will set a pattern of prosperity in all areas of your life.

Day 7: Believe and Receive

Build your self-confidence and believe in the possibility of potential customers, soul mates, healing, finances, health, balance, family, and all the above. You will manifest it, if you believe!

If you look back at your life and make a kind of inventory of the people you have known, you may recognize a kind of pattern. Either people have supported you, or they have shut down your ideas. When you think of this second group, if you look back at their reasons, it is usually not because they want to punish you or fight you or take your passion away; it is usually because, in some way or another, they were afraid "for" you, or trying to protect you in the only way they knew how, which was to stop you from taking that step they themselves were too afraid to take toward their own goals. Often they didn't have the talent or imagination, and therefore could not see your potential. This does not mean that you don't have it; it just means that these people are tone deaf to your abilities. Just follow your passion, and do it anyway.

Part of the forgiveness frequency is learning to truly forgive those who have hampered you with what at the time may have felt like unsupportive behavior. Forgive them their negative notions, and move ahead without them. They will come around eventually. When you stand assured and positive, nothing can stand in your way.

Yes, Yes, Yes (Reinforce the Flow of Creativity)

What does your YES Frequency look like in your own mind? Reinforce the flow of your creativity by painting a picture in your mind – a kind of motion picture wherein you are the star and all that flows around you are the people, places, and things that you are working toward in life but in your meditation you *already have it!* Build a kingdom in your mind to pull from and go to. Pave the streets with your kind of gold. The Field of Dreams, wherein life is "as if"… and when you see it, it will come. Envisioning the results you want in your life and living "as if" can be your reality when inside The YES Frequency.

Mastering Your Emotions

Be positively prepared! Be prepared for the expected. And more importantly, be prepared for the unexpected. Become aware of how you are thinking about what goes on around you, about what you can see and what you can't see. Understand that "stuff happens," and maximize your ability to roll with the punches, because life can be a roller coaster of stress and it isn't always fun.

We are all subject to stress and unfortunate happenings in our lives. The question is not whether stress will occur, but when and how will we handle it. Some people go to pieces when confronted with the slightest problems, while others masterfully handle the most devastating circumstances.

Most of us fall somewhere between these two extremes, but we need to learn to handle our "crisis situations" in the most constructive and spiritual ways possible. If we can acknowledge those strong emotions that surge up in us during these stressful times (rage, guilt, fear, and so on), and neither deny or suppress them nor let them control us, but instead deal with them rationally, we will be stronger. In a clearer state of mind we will be able to identify and cope with our lives and the lives of others. Denying or suppressing these strong emotions does not make them go away; on the contrary, they will come out in other ways, such as the onset of illness.

Trusting your unconscious mind is about trusting yourself. It's the most powerful way of being fully integrated with the mind, body, and spirit. It's discovering that you have within you an unlimited source of love, forgiveness, trust, balance, compassion, gratitude, and spirit. You will find this wisdom within yourself as you accept yourself and practice daily the experience of wholeness.

It is key that we learn to recognize the connections among our thoughts, attitudes, and responses to these crisis situations. In that way, we will not have an overreaction to a trivial event. When we are caught up in this pattern, we are using up a lot of unnecessary energy, which leaves us constantly drained and unprepared to cope with real emergencies. It is important for us to maintain a balanced perspective during emotional upsets. We must be objective about situations that we can do nothing about or could not have possibly prevented. We must also take responsibility for our actions in order to understand them and ourselves better and learn from them.

It is necessary to develop our self-awareness in order to spot the attitudes that cause the most confusion in our minds and the most stress inside. Our bodies must also be well nourished in order to rest and recuperate from a stressful siege: we must prepare both our bodies and minds to meet the stresses that we cannot avoid. Stress that is chronic or extreme may eventually disable you from life as you know it.

There are many methods that can help you manage stress, but without awareness or regulation of your mental habits, the strain will return in a short time and affect all areas of your life. You do not want to use these methods solely as stress-relief techniques; instead, alter those mental habits that are producing the stress syndrome in you. True transformation will occur once you master your emotions.

Unfortunately, we do not generally look for transformation. We wait until we find ourselves in a bad, uncomfortable place, and through the experience of being emotionally cornered we are forced to turn to another answer. All too often, it is through this experience that we discover transformation. Loneliness, isolation, the inability to get along with loved ones or friends – the list of things that may push us into a corner is endless.

Transformation usually deals with core issues. All we need to realize is that transformation means change, trust, and belief. We need to give up all of our old negative feelings, thoughts, and beliefs. You know the ones. They make you feel miserable and scared.

During deep, intense transformation, buried feelings and memories may surface. Some of the first feelings to appear may be sadness, fear, and disappointment. Recollections of physical or emotional abuse may arise. This can take a toll on your psyche.

Some of us are so good at denying our feelings, wants, and needs that we fool ourselves into thinking everything is okay. That is why it is common for people to say they don't know how they feel. As the work of transformation progresses, they discover repressed anger, rage, and self-sabotage within their feelings.

During periods of transformation, feelings can be erratic as you try to examine the reasons why "I feel so bad!" Or in the other respect, reasons why "This makes me so happy!"

During the transformation process, as these buried feelings, emotions, and judgments surface, take the techniques you've learned to forgive and heal them. Validating the deep work is essential in order to heal and be completely free. We must work with positive repetitive strategies in order to move into The YES Frequency, thus creating divine synchronicity.

Control yourself, and master your emotions, your thoughts, and your actions. If you have a spiritual or religious life and stay connected to what you consider your source, you will have what you need to cushion the blow of most disappointment or loss. If you are working out regularly, consuming a diet that is high in fiber and complex carbohydrates and low in sugar and fat, you will be prepared for the punches that life can throw at you.

Assess the damage, and begin to take back the power you have handed over to nervous tension in your life. While pressure is a normal part of life, we exacerbate its potentially harmful effects by focusing on the stress itself.

How many times have you complained, "I'm so stressed!" That only creates more stress. It's the same as when we're tired from overwork or lack of sleep. "I'm so tired," we repeat to ourselves and others – and pretty soon, we're more tired than we were when we started moaning about how tired we were to begin with!

It's also a way of focusing unnecessary attention on ourselves by turning the events of our lives into exaggerated drama. We make a big deal out of too many things, instead of taking them in stride and telling ourselves that we can handle what life hands us.

Before you step onto that stage, stop and take a deep breath, then assess the situation. Consider what you have power over and what you don't. Then take appropriate action. Sometimes it is also good to literally just "walk it off."

While the death of a loved one or a divorce is a devastating loss, if handled with grace, dignity, and consideration to all, the loss can be made more bearable. When your system is being nourished at every level, this will keep you in the purification frequency and help you master your emotions.

That said, allowing yourself to fall apart is natural and can be a healthy, acknowledging way to heal. Having the comfort of friends and family and leaning on your own spiritual beliefs is beneficial. When you view stressful events not as the end of the world but as another opportunity to show up for others and for yourself, you will be able to achieve an emotionally healthy state of thinking.

We must continue to feed ourselves that which supports us and keeps us healthy. "Life on life's terms" will not be some foreign phrase, but a concept that enables us to accept what life has to offer, while exercising the true power we have over ourselves and our reactions.

The Positive Use of Meditation

Meditation is the science of deep breathing and silence-relaxation. It is a form of healing and the art of listening to the spirit of the word. The purpose of daily meditation is to open your inner vision and third eye. What this sixth chakra provides is a stress-reducer that produces psychophysical changes and has been repeatedly validated in clinical trials by medical and psychological professionals worldwide.

There are many forms of meditation. Records on meditative practices date back two thousand years.

Breathing exercises have been part of the teachings of yoga for many centuries. Yogis have used this discipline to control their body and mind and to develop their mental, physical, and spiritual strengths.

You will experience immediate benefits from breathing deeply, but you must practice daily to appreciate its full effects. Deep breathing gives you a feeling of great relaxation. Remember to breathe through your nose and practice good posture. Develop your own program of deep breathing or yoga exercises to release your tensions; this will stimulate your circulation and nervous system, make you more alert, give you more energy, relieve your tension and sinus headaches, and help you cope with stressful life situations.

Meditation can be the best gift of love and nurturing you give your body, mind, and soul. It is another way to reconnect with your soul, your inner self, and your higher self – a way of awakening your inner knowing and your true nature. It is a way to transcend your pain, hurt, anger, fear, and all other negative energies. It is a way to know and listen to the message your body and soul are giving you. Through meditation you can get in touch with the flow of infinite energy, healing, love, and joy. Meditation is an experiential exercise.

The word "meditation" itself is very interesting. The Latin *meditara*, "to ponder," is supposed to be from the same basic root as *mederi*, "to heal"; the Aryan root of both these words is *Madh*, "to learn," from *ma*, or *man*, "to think, to wish, to call upon, to stay."

Many studies have shown consistent neurophysiologic patterns that occur during meditation, including a slowing of the breath and heart rate, which decreases the rate of oxygen consumption and reduces blood pressure and metabolic rate. This reduction can be greater than after six hours of sleep, according to some physiologists. Meditation not only can be used to reduce blood pressure but to help stabilize it.

Set aside a block of time each day, and commit to practicing your daily meditation without interruption. The key to a great result is intention and consistency. Do what feels right and works in your busy schedule. Even if you only meditate for ten minutes every day, it will help. Some people experience better sleeping habits after meditating for a while.

Transcendental Meditation™ is the registered name for a Siddha Yoga approach to meditation brought to the world by Maharishi Mahesh Yogi in the late 1960s. A simplified approach with a mantra is given to initiates, along with techniques and instructions for their use. This approach, emphasizing human potential and scientific evaluation, has deemphasized the religious connotations of Hinduism to a great degree. The meditator places himself in a state where he is undistracted by either external or internal stimuli. The goal is to gain mastery over "attention."

I meditate early in the morning, throughout the day – even in just five-minute intervals – and, when needed, again sometimes at night. No matter where I go or what I do during the day, I am consciously aware of getting in the meditative state to quiet my mind and my emotions, so that I can be fully present for each of my work sessions.

5

The Frequency Of
Your Words

Language matters. I earlier mentioned the power of what you "literally say," and how it serves as an active force in your life. Every complaint you have can be changed by the power of thinking: "YES, I can. YES, I am. YES!"

Let's change your mind as to how you nourish your thoughts. Let's think powerful positive thoughts. Let's embrace the best of you and take your life and celebrate an ability you already have: to take control of your center of operations, which is your mind.

Clear your mind, and understand that every word you utter should have a positive influence over you, those around you, and your inner thoughts. Fine-tune your vocabulary! Give your mind a break by eliminating all negative thoughts and expressions.

The Language of Miracles

When you maintain discipline over your literal use of words, you maintain control over your negative or positive frequency. When you are aware of the significance you inject into your everyday life, and how it derives from the words you use, you will become an example to others of how to use language appropriately. By eliminating any opening to put yourself or others down you will stay positive, creating a balanced state where you have eliminated the need to keep yourself in a "less than" or "not good enough" state.

If you are a parent, you will particularly feel the impact of this change in self-expression, as your children will find your words much more encouraging and inspirational.

Managers, too, will find this different application of language a formidable tool for positive change. You will see results immediately. Co-workers will be energized without even knowing why. Remember: you can't take back your words, and no apology will ever soothe the wounds caused by negative or careless words. Words can impress themselves deeply into the psyches of others, so choose them wisely. Words are especially powerful in the mouths of those in teaching positions. Positive, reinforcing language provides the kind of effective encouragement that will help students and children achieve greatness. The words that those in positions of authority use have the ability to have a lasting impact on a child's thinking, to move them forward or stop them in their tracks. Success in The YES Frequency means being aware every day of your life of the impact you have on others through the language you use.

Test Your Language

Take a moment and check the language you are using. Is your inner voice chastising? Is that inner voice mimicking some negative training that you absorbed in earlier years? Is a parental voice that is echoing some negative language from childhood? Or is the inner voice imitating an ex-partner from a relationship that was riddled with judgment?

The language you use requires you to carefully monitor your thinking. The words you choose will take on a life of their own, so clean up the words you use to describe anything and every-thing, especially yourself!

Eliminate the following negative self-statements:

I'm not...

I'm useless...

I can't...

I'm broke...

I'm too fat...

I'm too old...

I'm not enough...

Eliminate the following negative thought patterns:

If only...

Why can't I?...

They won't let me!...

And for you self-deprecating comedians who are extremely good at making fun of yourself: please think about changing the humor UP! Yes, it is funny when you lead in to jokes with phrases like, "What do I know?" "I've got one foot in the grave." "I'm so useless that..." Take note: This is delicate terri-tory, and you should be cautious of saying these things about yourself.

Instead, if you are "financially challenged," better to make a joke that reveals the humor in a challenging situation. For example, instead of saying "I'm so broke I can't afford to go anywhere or do anything," state:

- I do need to ask my chauffeur if the Learjet is ready.

- I must reply to this text — it's from the President.

- Let me see if my executive assistant can clear me for that telephone call.

Even in jest, you can mark yourself in ways the universe will recognize. The universe can and does hear you. Be a productive influence on your frequency. Every day, you can hear people using words that help create and define their lives. However funny, negative jokes and insults do nothing but perpetuate noninspirational results.

Be aware of the words that you use during the course of any given day. Use constructive humor, whenever possible.

Create daily inspiration by changing your mental atmosphere. Using the commitment key format, try writing out some key issues you may be experiencing, then turn them around into a positive commitment key.

Here are some examples. Read them aloud and then create your own:

Commitment Keys

YES, I hold the key to everything.

Take your key with you, and it will remind you to stay in your unlimited power of YES, so that all that it encompasses will be at your side.

YES, I will prevail.

Truly knowing that YES is the answer is what will enable you to gain control of your life. You will no longer feel that you are spinning out of control. No one will be able to push your buttons. Balance and harmony will be in your marrow.

YES, I can find my center.

There may be days that test your ability to stand in the center of the unlimited YES Frequency. Until you have been practicing this ritual for some time, you may need to lean on your personal key code or employ breathing techniques, so that you can't be knocked off balance. Just know that once you find your center, like a dancer, no one can knock you off kilter.

YES, I share power in a place of warmth.

Once you master your place in the frequency, the inviting feeling of warmth from the sun will pour from you. You will be the "go-to" person for advice. And there will be many people who cross your path whom you will assist toward other helpful positions in life. You will be the guide who shares your story and helps others to find the place of warmth inside themselves. You will be strong enough to find peace and resolve and strong enough to share this ability, so that others, too, can evolve to a greater place of inner contentment.

YES, I am all expressions of love in all that I do and say.

Today my entire being is open and ready to receive all that is well. I am standing in success in all areas of my life. Every day, giving thanks for all my blessings and spiritual knowledge is a ritual way of thinking for me. Staying present and perfect in a healthy life is my mantra. I allow life to flow through me and those around me, bringing new events for me to experience. Letting go of the old and welcoming the appearance of the new is what I strive and stand for.

Your continued commitment to compassion and kindness is an avenue that will give you answers. Trust that you are superb. Your ability to create changes that you are proud to stand by will place you on the fast track to living inside The YES Frequency and reaching all that it has to offer.

Overcoming Negative Self-Talk

Each day, each moment, we participate in an ongoing creative process as our thoughts and beliefs manifest our experiences. Your language is a key to positive change.

Focus on changing your language **from** a negative statement **to** a positive one. For example, change your language from a negative statement, such as "I am afraid of what is going to happen to me in the future," to a positive one: "I'm excited about what the future will bring me."

Here are a few more examples of **from** and **to** statements:

From: "I can't afford to buy those shoes."
To: "I choose not to buy those shoes."

From: "I can't afford to go to Europe."
To: "At this moment I choose not to go to Europe, because I'm very busy."

From: "I can't buy the refrigerator I want because I am broke."
To: "I choose not to buy that refrigerator because I'm waiting for the newest one to hit the showroom floor."

From: "Even though I want an iPad like my friend's, I can't buy one.
To: "I choose not to buy an iPad now, because I'm waiting for the new iPad with all the latest gadgets and applications."

You want to rephrase not only your words but all the thinking that the words stem from. Align this thinking with your mission statement. This takes practice! Rome was not built in a day! You want to choose and use your words carefully, but don't go off the charts picking something too unattainable. Remember that when you set unrealistic expectations of yourself, you are setting yourself up for failure in your own mind.

For an example of how to alter your mind pathways with words, let's return to the idea of fear of change. We want to leave the fear (which is not real) behind. When you change fear statements into empowered statements such as "I am not afraid of making changes in my life," this is when the real changes start to ignite.

Examples of FROM – TO:

From: "I'm never going to have it..."
To: "I can have exactly what I want..."

From: "If only I had more money..."
To: "I always have the money to do and have what I choose..."

From: "I hope I get the opportunity..."
To: "I accept great opportunities..."

From: "Moving and change scare me."
To: "I'm excited about moving and the big change."

From: "Will I ever find a good job?"
To: "I have a great new job!"

From: "I never feel lucky."
To: "I am very lucky!"

From: "I'm not sure I can do it..."
To: "I can do anything..."

From: "I doubt I will meet my life partner."
To: "I have a great life partner who supports my great-ness."

Keep the Application of the Sun technique from the earlier chapter with you, and use "YES" repetitions to help maintain your frequency and achieve endless positive results. Doors will keep opening in your life. Staying in the frequency depends on how much you want to live with "attainment."

When facing challenges, use the sun technique to help you stay in the frequency. This calm inner strength will bring your exterior a true, balanced control over all issues.

Use the following template as a guide as you create your own consolidated formula for Values, Mission Statement, and Affirmations. Feel free to write this down, if you need a hard copy to help you stay on track in keeping to the frequency.

VALUE

If your highest value is "happiness within a career":

MISSION STATEMENT

"I AM creative and experiencing great miracles in all areas of my life."

AFFIRMATIONS

YES, I am an intelligent, able, and confident person.

YES, I am worthy of being loved and respected.

YES, I am a whole and complete person.

ACTION ITEMS

List all the things that you've always wanted to do in order of priority. Believe and trust in yourself. Visualize yourself in action.

Trust

Trust is what allows us to have meaningful relationships with other people, and even with ourselves; without it, we cannot converse without wondering whether the person we are talking to is speaking honestly.

The decision to trust yourself is a choice you make. We have all made what we perceive as mistakes, and each of us could probably come up with a number of reasons why we supposedly shouldn't trust our own judgment. If we stay in that space, we are choosing to limit ourselves. And that's the choice we need to consider. Do we want to exist in a space that creates unnecessary emotional, physical, and experiential limits? No. We want to free ourselves of all self-imposed restrictions and open our life to endless potential.

When you make the choice to trust yourself, it's important to make sure that your trusting affirmations are supported in your cellular beliefs all the way and to include your values.

Wholeness means entirety. Trust is an opening to renovation. That transformation is available to us all. Activate taking action into believing and having faith that YOU ARE ENOUGH, that from now you will stay in TRUST with yourself. As long as you have carried your mission statement and your valued "want" forward, along with all the layers up to this point, you are secure to move forward in trust knowing:

YES, you will find that new job.

YES, you are looking forward to a healthy relationship.

YES, you envision your work being honored.

And when you are in a meeting at that new job, those who meet you will be inspired by your optimistic outlook, and you will find your new job to be exactly as you have been envisioning it. The frequency of your words will affirm trust, and all its energy will help you to meet your life partner. Or, if you are in a relationship, it will be refueled with light and love because your heart will be lifted with a new, energetic passion for life, which will be very intoxicating to your other half.

And when you live with trust, abundance, and thoughts of gratitude, the financial aspects of life will burst with opportunity. You will find you have enough time and energy to do more than you have ever accomplished before. Your trust in yourself will lead you to overflow with creativity.

Your trust and love for yourself will be visible, just like a fresh car wash. Have you ever noticed that your car usually drives better when it's clean? Or how, when it rains, all the buildings and streets look newer? How the air is fresher, with a feeling it has been newly oxygenated, after a good rainstorm? The same is true for your train of thought.

Humor me, and try this simple test. This one is designed for the experimentalist.

Go look in a mirror! Yes, bend the page in this book and go get a mirror, or ask someone to bring you one. Borrow a friend's compact. Go to a mirror stand and take a deep breath.

Okay. Now look in the mirror. Gaze in your eyes. And simply say YES! Acknowledge the smile in your eyes. Recognize the feeling in your heart. YES is accompanied by good feelings, an open heart, and a subtext of willingness in your thoughts.

Okay. Now look in the mirror and say NO. Do you feel the block – the instant wall that is built? Certainly, there are useful moments in life where the word NO is necessary. But for the intents and purposes of this lesson in fruition, I need you to store that word in the outskirts of your mind.

When you are next spending time with friends, just try this test with them. Look in their eyes as they say both words, and you will see the difference. You can actually feel the positive influences entering your vibrations when you simply say YES! YES resonates like certain music that moves us to joy. YES will detoxify the past treadmill of negative thoughts that have blocked your dreams and goals from being realized.

Just as fast food, preservatives, refined sugars, and stress have effects on your body's ability to digest properly, you need to feed your mind with the right thinking to lift your mood. Focus your mind on positive pathways like:

YES, my positive attitude reigns.

YES, everything will work out for the highest good.

YES! I accept my past and understand how it has shaped my life today!

No matter what has transpired in your life, no matter what difficulties you have gone through to get you where you are today, clearing the negative blocks is essential in order to move forward in your life. It is all in how you look at it, and this alone will move you from mediocrity to courageous change. You are unique and have a voice to give life and thought and compassion to others.

YES! I let go of the old and open my heart to let the new appear!

When you truly let go of all negative thoughts, everything feels better and lighter and joy starts to rule your day. When you sink into this frequency of YES, it will introduce you to new opportunities and people.

YES! I am an expression of love!

Living as an expression of love and speaking with the words and intonation of love brings love right into your life. Just like a winning lottery ticket, you are richer than you were before. People will find themselves saying YES to you!

YES! My entire being is open and ready to receive all that is good!

Staying open and using the language of this technique is a way of life that will give you opportunities that you would never have had the occasion to encounter had you not been inside this frequency of YES.

> YES! I see beyond my fear and live a joyous and prosperous life!

You will be an eyewitness to your own life changing so much that you will want to share the wealth. Do yourself a favor and *be* the difference; don't preach it. Being an example of success will have people clamoring to know what you have been doing and what your new secret is. Endless possibilities will start coming at you, left, right, and center.

You will also recognize this YES Frequency in others. You will gravitate to them, and they will in turn be leaning toward you for the same positive reasons. These will be the kinds of people who want to work with you.

If you are having a bumpy day, and the bicycle handlebars of life are getting wobbly, hang onto these affirmations.

> YES! I feel the warmth of the sun in the word YES.

Go to your meditative state of "YES" and recall the warmth of the sun and the warmth of the warm water pouring over you and say, "YES." It will push out the negative so you can stay on track.

Eventually you won't even need to close your eyes; you will radiate love from your eyes with a knowing understanding that will cause people to stop any negativity toward you in a heartbeat.

> YES! I am transcending my goals toward my destination.

This transformation will infiltrate every part of your life. Everyone in your address book – family members and loved ones, your coworkers, and everyday acquaintances – will feel your "YES" radiating. This is the key that will enable you to make choices that you have never known before. I guarantee your family and friends will be taking notice of the tone of your voice, and it will change how they react to you in a more loving and nurturing way.

YES! My clarity of desire will fulfill my prophecy.

Being decisive about your wants and needs and making clear, definitive statements toward your goals will have the universe in line with what you want. This also means you must make clear steps toward that end result. Your destination is right in front of you. Take one step at a time to get there. Waiting for the stars to align is not going to get you to your final destination. You must follow through to fulfill your heart's desire and your personal prophesies.

YES! All thoughts provoke the light within me to shine.

Your thoughts are your own personal glowing screen or, if you are inclined toward a more traditional metaphor, think of a flashlight that shines within you.

The clarity of "YES" sheds light on a situation; it gives lucidity of information that will bring forward your valued "want" and that will consolidate data so that you can make a proper strategy of what is to be done. When you illuminate your mind with a positive and clear train of thought, you ignite your entire being to perform in a positive, loving, "YES" fashion. This will pave the way to your future.

> "What you see in others has more to do with who you are than with who other people are."
> – Epictetus

Sustaining Your Confidence

Place your confidence on a pedestal! My pedestal exercise is one in which you envision your confidence standing before you on a pedestal, rather like an award that sits on your fireplace mantle. It's a gentle reminder that your confidence is an accomplishment that took a great deal of thought and work to achieve.

Your confidence is an invisible badge that you wear, much like, back in the day, a sheriff in an Old West town wore his star to show that he represented "The Law." Wear your confidence in that way.

When you own this practice of feeling your "panache," it will enable you to follow through and those that surround you will feel your ability to lead. This is an integral trait to acquire. Maintaining self-assurance brings forth an "enlightened" impression inside and out.

Along with your clear vision and positive pronouncements, it is imperative to be genuine in your confident state of being. You can't maintain your "programming" unless you are aware of this. Stay in the frequency and allow yourself to soar!

Continue doing, thinking, and practicing all the new beliefs and you will sustain your confidence, keeping you in The YES Frequency. Remember the quote in Chapter 4: "An unmanaged mind will always return you to your old beliefs"? Your mind is just like your body – if you give up exercising, it will lose tone. Feelings are a reflection of your ongoing state of mind. Whatever your vision is, it is an expanded version of you. Be confident in your vision and in yourself.

Step into your frequency of *self-love through embodying confidence in everything you do and touch*. We have been given dominion over all that is, and all that is thought. Take your vision by the hand and escort it to where you want to be with self-assuredness.

Life Key Code

Life flows through you. You will always be the one who decides how to use the power of YES, where it is directed, and the results it will produce.

Part Three
Living Your Vision

6

The Intuition Frequency

Intuition is the indescribable feeling of "knowing." We all have at least one story of the use of "intuition," where it seemed to stand front and center in our lives. It may have been after an incident of sorts – a time before or after the event that you recalled, reflected upon as a kind of "inner warning" or a "recognition" that only became apparent after a certain situation presented itself.

Some of these times we remember fondly: "I knew the minute I met her, she was the one." However, sometimes what seems like intuition is really just fear-based thoughts in your mind. Because they feel similar to the gut feelings we sometimes get, I call these "fear-based intuitions." They are not pure intuition. "I just had this feeling to stop. It was then that I warned my friends to stop on the trail." If these intuitions are from "pure intuition" and not fear-based intuition, you understand the gift.

The Gift

Everyone possesses intuition. Instinct and awareness are insights you were born with. But due to the inundation of outside influences over time, the inner gift of intuition gets buried deeper and deeper with age. Finding your own gift of intuition is about listening to the healthy inner voice deep inside you.

If you were fortunate enough to be born into surroundings that embodied the balance of love and a calm, steady, and healthy environment, you will already be way ahead in accessing your gift of intuition. When a child is raised with care and honor and respectful, balanced love, and their infant wants are listened to, the child learns to more readily adapt to taking care of him or herself. This comes from being at ease and having confidence in the parenting that surrounds him or her. This child is ready and able to project his or her own healthy frequency into the universe; it just is an innate talent.

Children are like sponges – they soak up everything around them. Parents all too often underestimate what their children understand, even from the time of birth. Think back to your own upbringing, because it's there you will find keys to the why of where you are now. As you recognize that you have emotions traveling through your body in every moment, try and note the patterns of teaching that they were birthed from.

While your emotions are a necessary and beautiful part of you, you are not your emotions – you're much more than that. Your emotions are tools for you, but they are not in charge; you're the one who's in charge. Your emotions play the role they were meant to, i.e., allowing you to feel and experience your own humanity, from the most difficult end of the spectrum to the most enjoyable. But they don't run your life; *you do.*

Tapping into the frequency of your gift allows you to enjoy a lasting peace with yourself. Become conscious that the gift is within each and every one of us. Keep listening inward. The constant, broad, and mindful perspective of your intuition is contained within everything you do.

Miracles and possibility always come hand in hand with love; this is the frequency path to mastering your emotions.

Forgiving and loving people just flow – nothing seems to bother them, nothing stands in their way; people are always attracted to their frequency. These progressive individuals create incredible lives for themselves.

This way of being embodies "the gift." Truly, this gift is like your own personal "money tree." You will reap an endless supply of "choices" when you adhere to the promise of owning your own gifts. Trusting your inner self leads to a truly calm and focused individual. It all goes back to the thoughts affecting the decisions you make.

I want to remind you that when you choose to forgive, one of the greatest rewards you receive is returning to the state of living fearlessly. You will feel empowered in speech and expression, instead of afraid. You will move fearlessly though your life, confident in your own experiences, your wisdom, and your growth, and above all, confident in the miraculous frequency of love. This is a gift to accept and enjoy forever; like air, it never runs out. It will move you forward, rather than leaving you stuck in a swirling past.

Acknowledging your gift and listening will catapult you forward into your new life. You can direct it in whichever way you want. You can even allow this positive energy to direct you.

The YES Frequency is absolutely weightless, and you are now free to decide where to take and invest yourself. This gift is your life force – your soul's force. It's a knowledge that empowers and strengthens you. It brings synchronicity.

Again, when you give yourself permission to forgive, you are giving yourself permission to heal. This is another one of the greatest gifts you can give yourself. Imagine the liberation that comes with letting go. By forgiving, you set yourself free. You no longer carry that heavy load with you. You no longer walk around with cords strapping you to other people. You return to your natural state of being, the truest essence of you. The anger and resentment have been cleansed; all the baggage has been washed away.

Move lightly, openly, and with a clear state of purpose into the rest of your life. Be like a child in purity of consciousness, truly free again.

Step Into the Process

How does a nonintuitive person learn to be intuitive? Intuition is a part of our nature. It is an integral skill with which we are born as spiritual human beings. Babies and young children are spontaneously intuitive: they know and sense energy and recognize what is around them at all times. They move toward that which feels good and safe and loving ... and away from that which feels negative or stressful. Unless traumatized, they are trusting and open and willing, using intuition as their guidance mechanism, until at some point in childhood, like damaged software on a computer, this intuitive skill is socialized out of them. In a variety of ways, they are told that what they perceive is not quite right, that what they are feeling and sensing is socially incorrect or wrong. It is at this point, in our earliest days, that we often begin to doubt our intuition; we second-guess ourselves and begin to phase out the routine and natural use of our gift of intuition.

Given this, it should make sense that the process of using our intuition is one of remembering, becoming familiar once more with the process that is, and always has been, our internal compass and our natural state.

First, quiet the mind...

The first phase of rekindling our intuition is to raise our vibration and frequency. The best way to do this is to meditate. Meditation solidifies our connection to the universe.

One of the many benefits of a meditation practice is that of enhanced focus. In meditation, we go into that quiet, deep space of silence and simply allow our connection to God/the

Source to *be*. We become more attuned to the divine universal energies, which also allows us to feel who we are, and to be more in tune with ourselves, to distinguish our own energy from that of others, and to understand how to utilize this energy toward healing. Meditation, and the ensuing side effect of increased focus, allows us to identify and utilize our own energy in service to the divine, ourselves, and others.

Connect with heart energy

We want to stay in the luminous energy of our heart! Heart energy enables us to find our true, authentic inner voice on our divine path in life. Through meditation, focus, and resonance with the heart energy, we learn to identify what this inner voice sounds and feels like and how it expresses itself. Living in the heart experience of being deeply connected to God/Source, constantly residing in the heart energy, which is love, again connects us to that which we truly are, that which we express, and that which we deserve.

Use an invocation/affirmation

Another step in the process of reconnecting with our intuition is using an invocation or an affirmation: making a clear, concise statement and declaring our willingness to be open to receive pure, clean, clear intuitive information from the highest God/Source. Affirm again and again: "YES, I can!"

Receive the information

If you want to send an intention, such as an intention to find a good man or find a publisher, learn to trust the Download (the information that comes to you intuitively).

Experiment with this daily. Think of an intention. Keep it simple, be very clear. Send good energy or thoughts to a person, or send an intention to create a simple event. Carefully observe the results.

A crucial skill in using intuition is to learn how to receive the Message. Sit and listen. (This is the "ON" switch of intuition.) Observe the results, rather than attempting to control the experience or the outcome. Do not "think" about it; this is not an intellectual process. Trying to make it reasonable or analytical is the "OFF" switch.

To practice in the beginning, write down the messages you receive (quickly and without censorship or analysis). You can also record information verbally, or simply remember what comes through to your awareness, making a note of it to yourself.

Physical sensations are another method of receiving intuitive guidance. The body is like your "radar." If it is healthy and in tune, the body never lies. It is important to keep the body well tuned, like a fine instrument, so that it can do its best job. Treat it with care and consideration. It can react to a person, a place, a thing, an environment, an atmosphere, a particular food, an object – all of which gives us valuable information about any of these places, people, or things. Some of the things our body picks up may come through in sensations (heat, cold, chills, breathing changes, any of multiple subtle physical indications).

Sometimes intuition messages will transfer through objects. I remember one occasion when I was helping a friend pack for a move. We were just talking about his new house, when I picked up a crystal ashtray; suddenly, I felt a strong energy of a woman who was a lovely person, and I felt that she had died from smoking and consequently lung cancer. Spontaneously I said, "This belonged to someone who had cancer." My friend was taken aback and exclaimed, "Oh my God, that was my favorite aunt. Yes, she loved to smoke, and yes, unfortunately that was the catalyst to her death."

Intuitive information can come in many forms, in addition to physical sensations. We also have an emotional thermostat, which supports our intuition through a "feeling," or a sense of "knowingness" about a person, place, or thing. This information can come in the form of instant emotional states, images, visions, or ideas. We may instantly have a sudden emotional reaction to someone, to something, or to an environment or location. This can be subtle and rapid, a quick flash of recognition, or it can be pervasive and powerful, almost overwhelming when it happens.

Dreams can also offer us another avenue for powerful intuitive messages. They can be windows to detailed scenarios filled with valuable information, or they can be precognitive messages to which we need to pay special attention. Dreams are intense vignettes of intuitive material from which we can deeply benefit, if we simply learn how to read the messages.

One of my clients has "image boarding" talents, which is something she sees when she closes her eyes. She describes it as: "... rather like storyboards for a book or film. When I'm in a state of relaxation, pure intuitive messages come to me. It can be in the plain of day, early in the morning, or as I'm about to turn off the light to go to sleep. My eyes are closed and I am able to see black-and-white images, much like a projector from an old film sequence, or like a roll of black-and-white celluloid film negatives. Images roll before my eyes, giving black-and-white silhouettes. Description shapes to people, places, and things have presented themselves, giving me intuition, via preview, to people, places, and happenings."

This client's "image-boarding" talents enable her to see the future through fragmented imagery. This is a rare but pure intuition source.

My client Eileen had a business for around a year and a half on the 106th floor of New York's Twin Towers. Six of her working team were to have a meeting at 9 a.m. on the morning of September 11, 2001. The day before the intended meeting, Eileen had such a strong and foreboding feeling that she rescheduled the meeting, telling everyone to meet at a hotel restaurant approximately twenty blocks away. That morning at 9 a.m., she and her working team were overwhelmed by the fact that her intuition had saved all of their lives from the most devastating attack on the United States of America to date. Eileen has a rare gift of pure intuition.

Negative Messages

As we learn to receive messages through our intuition, keep in mind that we are learning to trust the universe. There is a flow of information and divine energy that supports our highest good, if we simply allow it to do so. In the practice of intuition, we learn to listen clearly, and to distinguish important messages from those associated with desire or fear. Desire, want, neediness, or fear are *not* intuition; they are functions of our ego.

Our ego is not a bad thing, and it certainly has a useful function in some aspects of our life. However, any negative messages that pop into our awareness accompanied by anxiety, criticism, or high stress are most often a product of the ego or interference from our outer world. Intuition, even when attempting to warn us about something dangerous or unwise for us, will present the information in a calm and clear manner.

A warning of danger or avoidance can feel quite strong and invoke feelings of fear. Keep in mind that a message of this nature can range from the most delicate, subtle of signs to the most blaring and forceful. However, this is to aid us, to guide us. Our pure intuition will present this information in a clear manner so that we can understand it! It is up to us to learn how to distinguish messages of warning and pure intuition from those of fear. We must go back into the knowingness of the heart energy vibration, so that we can eliminate fear and read the signs clearly.

When I was offered a television series at Fox Studios with my lawyer and producer, we met the executives for a series that they wanted me to host. I was truly looking forward to being a part of something rather cutting edge at the time. When we walked in the room and met these individuals who were presenting the show idea, before they even spoke – literally right after their introductions – red lights suddenly went off inside my mind. I received strong warning messages to *not* engage. It was such a strong feeling urging me *not* to do this project that I walked away from the show. I myself was taken aback by the feeling of intuition.

In the end, they went ahead and packaged not only one but a host of people, and what was produced was filled with sensationalism; it had absolutely nothing to do with honoring what I know to be spiritual thinking. Naturally, I was filled with gratitude that I had received the message not to engage.

Signs and Symbols

In addition to physical signals from our bodies, messages from the universe can arrive as a diverse array of signs or symbols. These messages can be visual, such as if you see a quote or a statement in some unexpected place. Or they can involve sighting a certain number, a specific letter, an object (you look on the ground, and in front of you is a feather or a coin); a sign (literally signs and billboards that you pass on the street, containing words or statements), license plate words or numbers, animals or pictures of animals. These incidents can validate that you are on the right path.

Synchronicity

Keep in mind that when you tap into universal consciousness – which is what you do when you use your intuition – you are able to access information that not only aligns you with the present moment but also with the past or future. Your intuition can even lead to an experience of *déjà vu* – a feeling of having been here before, merging in some mystical way with the same experience or the same people or the same location.

I have asked many people about their déjà vu experiences, and have been surprised to learn that some people claim to have *never* experienced any. Delving further, I found that those who said that they had never experienced déjà vu, didn't believe it to be an actual experience, or considered it to be simply the misfiring of a synapse in the brain, had one thing in common: they were all lost in their lives.

I want to write more about déjà vu at a later date, because it is an expression of underlying synchronicity, the connection of seemingly nonrelated or noncausal experiences, the universe's way of validating your intuition. Déjà vu has been a companion my whole life. I have had a strong feeling of déjà vu in all the countries I've taught in. In each city, I feel like I am stepping into part of my historical past. It is as if I have lived there before. This déjà-vu understanding has also led me in directions and to people who have remained prominent in my life.

Focus

Developing your intuition will enhance your ability to focus and take action in your daily life. Make it a regular practice. What is it that you intend to do and accomplish throughout the day? What are your goals, aspirations, dreams, and desires? Keep the focus on accomplishing one thing at a time, beginning with small goals and adding to them as each one gets checked off the list. Remember to focus on any intuitive information that comes your way while working and playing, noting any valuable details and validations that come back to you in the form of signs, synchronicities, and symbolic messages.

Action

Practice, practice, practice, and repeat the process. Creative activities are a good way to support relaxation of the mind, allowing a deepening receptivity to intuition.Music, art, dance, enjoying nature – these activities are all great vehicles through which our pure intuition can flourish.

Many creative people rely on their intuition, but all people use creative energy in some fashion, whether they are engaged in medicine, technology, mechanical endeavors, construction, design, or any of the infinite activities that occupy our daily lives, careers, hobbies, and recreational activities.

Stay open to the gifts of intuition. Incorporate the practice and awareness of using intuition into your daily life. Keep it simple and clear. Meditate. Focus. Take action. Remember this profound gift is your birthright. Through your heart energy, stay in touch with universal wisdom, and use it to stay true to the evolving path of your soul's expression.

Core YES Code

I expect new good into my life and welcome it when it arrives.

7

The Success Frequency

You now have all the tools you need to focus on what you desire. You are on your way to manifesting as fast as your thoughts. You have created the energy from your "valued want," drawing it into your energy field and magnetically attracting the mental situation you desire in your life.

At this very moment, you are building strength in your success frequency. The match is as perfect as the idea you created in your inner world through visualizing your life "as if." Once

> "The possibilities are numerous once we decide to act and not react."
> – George Bernard Shaw

the vibration and energy patterns of what you are choosing to create become a part of your daily frequency field, they will begin to transmit the frequency pattern of what you are manifesting on the physical plane, attracting it to you, and thereby manifesting it into being. Like an energy transmitter, you will be radiating that vibration outward, attracting what you desire and this end result into your life.

Behold, as the choices appear! Know that your entire being is now open and ready to receive all that is good! Affirm yourself with positive statements that tap into your YES Frequency:

> YES, I know that I can succeed in all areas of my life!
>
> YES, I give thanks for all my blessings and spiritual knowledge!
>
> YES, I am awake and alive and create perfect health!
>
> YES, I let life flow through my experience, bringing new events!
>
> YES, I let go of the old and let the new appear with love!
>
> YES, my entire being is open and ready to receive all that is good.
>
> YES, I am an expression of love in the success frequency.

Today is a new day. You're now ready to move forward, to release the burden of holding onto old beliefs that have kept you stagnant. It's a journey that will restore you to your natural state of being, one that will set you free. You are smack-dab in the middle of the frequency of your new life. To help keep you focused in this frequency, let's recap some of the information from earlier chapters.

Your Mission Statement is very important because it serves as your compass, pointing you along the path to the life you desire. Keep your mission statement and your goals in front of you at all times, and focus your energies on positively affirming what you want.   It is important to recognize what's been stopping you from forgiving yourself and others until now. If you've been holding onto anger toward yourself or someone else, there's a reason for it, and you need to address that reason before you can allow yourself to release old feelings. It's so vital to recognize that blockage and change it using the forgiving

> "Act as though you are and you will be."
>
> – Ernest Holmes

frequency. There's a part of you that knows and understands how to initiate "listening" to open up your pure intuition and "the gift" inside.

Life Key Code

Everything you have experienced in life has been generated out of you.

Building Your Ideal Life

Know that you are open to receive love – more than that, say it out loud: "I am open to receive love." Love connected to thought is like the musical score in a scene in a movie: it sets the tone for everything. The overture of your life will embody a grand feeling of inspired love, enhancing your success frequency.

Along with intention and vision and your mission statement for "What I want to have in my life," your life recipe includes love. Love is an energy and a vibration. If you want to have more love in your life, you need to give more love. And giving more love means you have to give more love to yourself. Remember that pushing into The YES Frequency is a culmination of all of the steps you have taken. These things are built for you! Accepting The YES Frequency is saying YES to yourself, so say it!

You may think that you don't have any love to give. But you do. Your thoughts have energy, an emotional charge, which connects to what you are thinking and doing in your life. Negative thoughts interfere with the vibration of love, so say "No comment" to your inner voice when it tries to criticize you. Use the soft words and tone you would use with someone you loved when you talk to yourself – because you should love yourself!

Every word that you speak is a step forward or backward along the path to the destination set out by your mission statement. As you walk this path, listen carefully to your footsteps. Picture yourself always and only moving forward – but if you do take a backward step, do not chastise yourself for it. This will only push you farther back! The things you are putting into your life should give you a clean feeling of freedom, not the clutter of the past. The forgiveness frequency means letting go of your guilt, your grudges, and all of the mistakes of the past you drag with you as you go forward in life.

Why do so many people cling to the past? We carry our stories with us all through our lives, but if you are still living with pain left over from past events, you need to allow yourself to let go. Why are you holding onto these old feelings? Have you bound your confidence and self-worth to things that happened long ago? Are you afraid to lose these things?

Confidence is built through everything you experience in your life, but you need to be proud of and love yourself *now*, for what you are doing, who you are becoming, and your entire being. Give yourself permission to love yourself now and the shackles of the past will fall away, leaving you open and free to resonate with the Frequency of YES.

Meditation practice is another way of honoring your body and bringing in the feeling of love. Take a deep breath and feel the vibration of love that is always within you. You are a manifestation of love. Really open up to more love, and take that feeling with you throughout your day. It's very simple: all you have to do is maintain it. There is no secret to accepting more love or becoming more love – just be it.

Visualization

Have you ever been in a place so removed from all the motion of life that you couldn't hear anything? No horns, no cell phones, no people talking in the background? Even inside your own mind? This is the perfect space for visualizing, free from distractions. You cannot hear the humming wings of a dragonfly over the rumble of a truck engine, and it's just as hard to manifest your energy to visualize what you want if you are distracted.

Close your eyes and allow yourself to see, sense, and feel yourself in your ideal scene. See yourself having what you would like, focusing on the details of your "want" and letting all else fall away. Think of the new house you will have and the sense of peace and security you will find there. Think of your heart beating fast as you meet eyes with your destined life partner for the first time. Think of your life "as if." Let the energy of your thoughts flow outward into the universe.

Step into your future. As you visualize your future experience, connect the emotional feeling of YES to this exercise. Do this once a day for the next twenty-one days. Do you remember playing with Legos as a child? This exercise of visualization and all of the layers we've worked through to this point are your Legos, building your life one brick at a time toward the "want" you desire.

Be conscious of your gratitude for today. So much of the time, people look back and focus on past events because they think they have nothing to look forward to. But the result of that is that they are not sending out positive energies about their desires, and their vibrations remain negative.

Why are you then surprised that positive events and people don't manifest? The universe is waiting to respond to you. You will only draw in what you send out. On the other side, people who focus on the future often waste too much of this focus on worry about their success or unpredictable events, and this sending out of negative energies draws them to a place they don't want to be in their life.

Be in the now. Remind yourself that each moment is precious, and be grateful for all of the things and people that are right in your life now. Take a deep breath and feel the present moment deep inside you. The present is where we manifest our desires and dreams for the future, and work toward them with our goals and missions statements, with every breath we take and every word we speak. Keep yourself in the now, and The YES Frequency will open to you, responding to your vibrations and carrying you into your most successful life.

The solid reality that we perceive as "real" is just one slice of the vast multidimensional universal and the many planes of existence. Where are our souls and energies in the physical plane of reality? All the ways our energies are working in the universe cannot be perceived by the five senses. Yet this is where change happens – with you radiating the energy of your desires, and the universe responding to that positive energy, as you magnetize good things toward you.

If you trust your higher consciousness you can create on the inner plane. Remember that things created on the inner plane manifest on the outer plane through the combination of the energy you radiate out into the universe and the events that are drawn to this energy. Tell yourself, "Any second now, miracles are going to happen in my life." If you truly believe it, they will. All that is required is to remain in The YES Frequency, vibrating in its success.

Afterword

These techniques and strategies will give you ways to bring positive results into your life. If you follow the simple and effective exercises detailed in this book, you will discover how to feel amazing throughout your life.

The YES Frequency aligns you with the universe in a way that propels you forward, engaging you in a successful vibration of endless choices.

Remember: You are always loved, supported, safe, and secure, and The YES Frequency is within you right now.

Say YES to life!

Success Stories

- One of my clients wanted a new hybrid car, and every time she passed one on the road, which was nearly every third car, she would say, "I'm happy for that person and I envision myself driving the same car." After eleven months, she had her new hybrid car.
- Another client had a history of relationships that, when I first met her, she described as, "It all went to hell in a hand basket." After using my techniques, she met not one man

but two men of her dreams, and had the decision of choosing who she wanted to start a relationship with.

- Yet another client had trouble saying no to people, and found herself not truly honoring herself and her talent. After using my techniques, she has never been in better shape. She now makes time for a vacation every year, which gives her a fresh perspective on her life and job and embodies "rejuvenation."

- One of my favorite stories is of a client who kept having metaphorical doors close on her face in terms of her projects and creative endeavors. After our private sessions she learned how to embrace those detours, and learned that what appears to be a negative is usually a profoundly positive opportunity for learning the lessons that these detours have to offer. She is now smack-dab in the center of where she wants to be and is thriving.

- One of my clients was a talent agent in Los Angeles who was exhausted from his job. He was always saying how much he hated LA, annoyed by this and that, and mentioned many times how much he wanted to move to Germany. During our session, I said, "Stop and think about what you are saying, what you are injecting into the universe. This negative spewing will only breed more of the same in your life." I instructed him to change his negative vernacular by saying instead "how much you love Los Angeles, and that you are looking forward to living and working in Germany." As soon as he changed his awareness, he manifested his dream within one year. He now rents out his LA home and lives in Germany, working in film in Berlin.

YES Affirmations for Successful Living

By saying the affirmations below out loud, as often as needed, you will uplift your frequency. Use repetition to incorporate them into your subconscious. Copy and paste them into your life.

APPRECIATION:
YES, today I recognize all my gifts, and know that I always have the right people around me.

FREEDOM:
YES, today I let go of all limitations.

POSITIVITY:
YES, today I only accept the best.

GENEROSITY:
YES, today my heart is full and open.

RELATIONSHIPS:
YES, today I accept that all my relationships are in complete balance and harmony.

FINANCES:
YES, today I accept an unlimited flow of stability and financial abundance.

BEAUTY:
YES, today I see how perfect everything is around me.

SELF-CONFIDENCE:
YES, today I can pursue anything with confidence.

ACCEPTANCE:
YES, today I am comfortable within myself.

KNOWLEDGE:
YES, today I attract great knowledge.

TRUST:
YES, today I trust myself, knowing that all my desires are fulfilled.

LOVE:
YES, today I stand in the knowing that love is all there is.

COURAGE:

YES, today I am exactly where I need to be.

"Affection is responsible for nine-tenths of whatever solid and durable happiness there is in our lives."
— C.S. Lewis

Acknowledgments

I am grateful to all those who have loved and supported me for many years, for your love has helped me discover my gifts and live my dream.

My infinite gratitude to Elyssa Davalos and Anne Taylor, for your insight and help with the completion of this book.

Thank you, Barbara Moulton and Rita Curtis, for your trust and commitment to my work.

Thank you for your help and expertise, Michelle Dotter and Amy Rennert.

Thank you, Findhorn Publishing. Special thanks to Gail Torr, Thierry Bogliolo, Sabine Weeke, Nicky Leach, and Carol Shaw for your support!

Thank you to all my wonderful publishers all over the world for your ongoing support and positive approach over so many years: Patrizia Santerini, Cristina Levy, Patty Gift, Judith Kendra, Jonathan Falcone, Sabrina Lescio, Timmy Falcone, Sabine Giger, Dynavision, Keiko Anaguchi, Yurika Yotsumoto, Ikuko Iwasaki, Rosanna Aronne and Amore Universo.

Special thanks to Evelyn M. Dalton, Patricia Q., and Judson Rothschild, for your constant love and support.

Thank you, Anita Gregory, for being an amazing friend and creative producing TV partner! Thank you, Drew Sherman at Sherman

Law Corporation, for all your amazing support.

Thank you, Ute Ville, for your friendship and photography.

I hope all the special people involved in my life are always acknowledged. I am grateful for your constant friendship and support. Thank you, Leeza Gibbons, Pili Montilla, Amelia Kinkade, Bruce R. Hatton, Michael Carey, Keith Cohn, Isabelle Von Fallois, Glennyce Eckersley, Beatrice Orlandini, Robyn Dvorak, Dr. Andrew DaLio, Doriana Mazzola, Sante Losio, Rachele Restivo, Cristina Unterberger, Donna Delory, Silvia Gavino, Davide Del Ninno, Nastassja Kinski, Gena Lee Nolin, Carrie Williams, Ralf Bauer, Nancy and John Clayburgh, Gina and Gregory McKay, Dottie Gagliano, Angela Croce, Marie-Luce and Laurent Le Febve de Vivy, Roland and Ursi Schafli, Veronica DeLaurentiis, Richard Ayoub, Nick Urbom, Sandy Ingerman, Emmanuel Itier, Asha Blake, Howard and K.O. Coones, Johnny Fratto, Jr., Angela Fratto, Alexis Fratto and Alyse.

Special thanks to: Bunim-Murray Productions; Jonathan Murray, Scott Freeman, Willis Robertson, Max Hirshik, David Berson, ITV USA Studios; Paul Buccieri, Bruce Robertson, Claudia Wong, and Joanna Cocuzzi and Ben Bitonti

Thank you, Deborah Arakelian, Kiki Melendez, Anna Ouroumian, Patricia Fleming, Laura and R.Q., Mairead Conlon, Maureen Driscoll, Peggy Moller, Shannon Factor, Traci Ireland, Amy Harris, Cheryl Welch Thomas, Marci Duff, Carol Waller, John Sofro, Annette Frehling, Jody Turner, and Caroline Bono.

> "The YES Frequency aligns you with the universe in a way that propels you forward, engaging you in a successful vibration of endless choices."
> – Gary Quinn

Recommended Reading

Bachman, Nicholai. *The Path of the Yoga Sutras.* Boulder, CO: Sounds True, 2011.

Beckwith, Michael Bernard. *Spiritual Liberation.* New York: Atria Books, 2008.

Braden, Gregg. *Deep Truth.* Carlsbad, CA: Hay House, 2011.

Chopra, Deepak. *Spiritual Solutions.* New York: Crown Harmony, 2012.

Di Martini, John. *Inspired Destiny.* Carlsbad, CA: Hay House, 2010.

Dyer, Wayne. *Wishes Fulfilled: Mastering the Art of Manifesting.* Carlsbad, CA: Hay House, 2012.

Hemingway, Mariel, and Bobby Williams. *The Willing Way: 10 Dynamic Steps for Connecting with Nature and Revealing Your Authentic Self.* Los Angeles, CA: Changing Lives Press, 2012.

Holmes, Ernest. *The Science of Mind.* Los Angeles, CA: Tarcher, 2010.

— *This Thing Called You.* Los Angeles, CA: Tarcher, 2007.

Lipton, Bruce. *The Biology of Belief: Unleashing the Power of Consciousness, Matter, & Miracles.* Carlsbad, CA: Hay House, 2008.

Millman, Dan. *The Four Purposes of Life.* Novato, CA: New World Library, 2011.

Rothschild, Judson. *Snap Out of It.* Los Angeles, CA:Create-Space Publishing, 2010.

Ruiz, Don Miguel. *The Four Agreements.* Novato, CA: Amber-Allen,1997.

Tolle, Eckhart. *The Power of Now.* Novato, CA: New World Library 1999.

Twyman, James. *The Barn Dance.* Carlsbad, CA: Hay House, 2010.

About the Author

International best-selling author, life coach, and television producer Gary Quinn shares his valuable insights and knowledge with a worldwide audience via his self-help motivational books, as well as audio CDs, TV and radio appearances, and numerous worldwide speaking engagements and seminars. His teachings have been embraced by people from all walks of life, including entertainers, athletes, and corporate leaders. Among his many clients are Academy Award winners, Grammy winners, and Olympic gold medal winners. His corporate clients include Mattel, Diesel, and The Indigo Corporation.

A highly regarded intuitive who works with the angelic forces, Gary is in demand worldwide for seminars, workshops, private sessions, and television host appearances. He frequently holds retreats and seminars in the United States, Switzerland, England, Japan, Ireland, Italy, Austria, Germany, Mexico, and Canada.

Gary has been featured in *Vogue* magazine, *Glamour Italy*, *Gala*, *Toronto Sun*, *Woman's Weekly*, *Red Magazine*, *Energie Magazine, Yoga Magazine*, *People*, *US Magazine*, *Reader's Digest*, and *InStyle Magazine*. He has appeared on Extra TV, NBC, FOX, BBC, ITV, Italia 1 & Rai TV, and on the radio with Leeza Gibbons and Shirley MacLaine.

Touchstone For Life Coaching Program®

Gary Quinn is the founder of the **Touchstone for Life Coaching Certification Program ®** and **The Angelic Intervention Program ®**, which train and transform individuals to create successful results in their lives. Gary Quinn and his certified coaches can help you to change your life. They offer workshops, classes, private coaching, keynote speaking, consulting, and training to become a certified Touchstone for Life coach.

To receive a free monthly newsletter and more information, visit **www.garyquinn.tv**

Join me on FACEBOOK and TWITTER

Touchstone for Life Coaching Program
P.O. Box 16041
Beverly Hills, California 90209 USA

A unique companion to the corresponding book by the same author, this motivational recording offers 101 affirmations for immediately improving one's life. Everyday words are used as mantras of healing—allowing for simple changes that lead to prosperity and happiness. Quinn's soothing yet confidant voice will put listeners at ease, allowing for an open and receiving state of mind. Acknowledging that 'no' signifies a sense of limitation, this audio CD eloquently captures the fields of possibility in 'yes' and gives practical guidelines for listeners to incorporate new attitudes in minutes.

Contents:

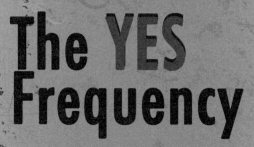

The YES
Frequency

*101 Affirmations
to Balance the Mind,
Body and Spirit*

GARY QUINN
author of
May the Angels Be with You

Accessible and effective, this succinct guide reveals a 28-day program designed to correct toxic behavior patterns so that readers can connect with their true essence. Positing that it takes 21 to 28 days to break old habits, this personal journey features a daily, channeled angel message for each step of the curriculum. Offering exercises, rituals, and case studies, this step-by-step process increases daily contact with personal angels and helps to form a more positive belief system, so that synchronicities and miracles become a standard part of life. Complete with meditations, real-life examples, and pragmatic suggestions for action, this dynamic tool is for anyone hoping to realize their dreams.

Pianist Isabelle von Fallois was diagnosed with a life-threatening form of leukemia. After fighting for life and death for 4 years she had a profound encounter with Archangel Raphael that changed her life forever and helped her to heal.

In the meantime she wrote several German and Italian bestselling books, recorded more than 50 meditations, developed the ANGEL LIFE COACH® Training and the ISIS ANGEL HEALING®, had her own radio show, was featured in lots of magazines and appeared on several DVDs, spiritual movies and German television.

The Power of Your Angels

28 Days to Finding Your Path and Realizing Your Life's Dreams

Isabelle von Fallois